Hearts & Dragons

Hearts & Dragons

The 4th Royal Berkshire Regiment
in France and Italy During the
Great War, 1914-1918

Charles R. M. F. Crutwell

LEONAUR

Hearts & Dragons: the 4th Royal Berkshire Regiment in
France and Italy During the Great War, 1914-1918
by Charles R. M. F. Crutwell

Originally published under the title
The War Service of the 1/4 Royal Berkshire Regiment (T. F.)

Published by Leonaur Ltd

ISBN: 978-1-84677-361-7 (hardcover)
ISBN: 978-1-84677-362-4 (softcover)

http://www.leonaur.com

Contents

Preface

This little work was undertaken at the request of Lieut.-Col. R. J. Clarke, C.M.G., D.S.O., while the war was still in progress. The Editor of the *Berkshire Chronicle* kindly gave it the hospitality of his columns in 1920. Its republication in book form is due to the generous support of Berkshire people; and I have been very fortunate in persuading Mr. Basil Blackwell to act as its publisher. The earlier portion is based on my own personal recollections, the latter on the war diary of the Battalion, which was admirably kept, and on information supplied by officers and men.

I have to thank Lieut.-Col. Ewen and Capt. Goodenough, M.C., for the trouble which they have taken to supply me with all available documents: and, among many others, Major G. A. Battcock, Captains W. E. H. Blandy, O. B. Challenor, M.C., G. H. W. Cruttwell, and Sergts. Page and Riddell for giving me personal details, and thereby clearing up many points which must otherwise have remained obscure.

The fortunes in battle of a small unit, like a Battalion, in the late war, can never make easy reading, but I hope that with the aid of the large-scale maps inserted in the text they may prove fairly intelligible. The Appendices are due to the present Adjutant, Capt. L. Goodenough, M.C.

CHAPTER 1

Mobilisation and Training

Late in the afternoon of August 2nd, 1914, the 4th Royal Berks Regiment joined the remainder of the South Midland Infantry Brigade for their annual camp on a hill above Marlow. War had broken out on the previous day between Germany and Russia, and few expected that the 15 days' training would run its normal course. It was not, therefore, a complete surprise when in the twilight of the next morning the battalion re-entered the same trains which had brought them, and returned to Reading. Soon after arrival, in accordance with orders received, the battalion proceeded to disband; but many of the men, unwilling to return to the distant parts of the county when further developments were confidently expected, remained at their respective armouries throughout that famous Bank Holiday. At last, at 7.20 p.m. on the next day, August 4th, the order for mobilisation was received, and conveyed throughout the county that night by the police and eager parties of volunteers. The plan of mobilisation had been closely studied in all its details, and worked with complete smoothness. By 2 p.m. on the 5th the assemblage at Reading was complete, and after a laborious day spent in medical inspection, drawing of equipment and of ammunition, 28 officers and 800 other ranks entrained in the evening for their war station at Portsmouth, while 2 officers and 65 other ranks remained at Reading to receive the transport from the remount depot. At Portsmouth three days were spent mainly in digging, until a new move on the 9th brought the whole of the South Midland Division together at Swindon. Here on the 14th the battalion was invited by telegram from the War Office to volunteer immediately for foreign service. At this date the formation of the new service units had scarcely begun, and few realised how widely the common burden of responsibility would be shouldered in the next few weeks. The question, therefore, arose naturally in many minds, why those whose patriotism had led them without encouragement and sometimes with derision to qualify for the defence of the country in peace, should be the first called upon to extend their statutory obligation when emergency arose. None the less, within a few days a large majority of the men, and practically all the officers, had volunteered. History will, I believe, honour this prompt decision and recognise its value.

On August 16th, the division entrained for Leighton Buzzard, and the battalion spent four days in billets at Dunstable, 8 miles away, before setting out on the 20th on a 70-mile trek to its final destination at Chelmsford. In spite of the heat, the dusty roads and the small opportunities afforded since mobilisation for practice in marching, the journey was successfully accomplished in four days. The inhabitants of Stevenage, Hoddesden, Waltham Abbey and Fyfield, where we billeted in succession, to whom the passage of troops was still a pleasing novelty, and the provision of billets more than a business transaction, received us with every kindness. Thus Chelmsford became the adopted home and theatre of training for the battalion, except for the period September 24th–October 16th, which was spent in three adjacent villages, Broomfield and Great and Little Waltham. The relations between the town and the soldiers were excellent throughout, and many warm friendships were made; while in the surrounding country the landowners and farmers made the troops free of their land, thereby greatly assisting the field training, which was carried on uninterruptedly through a fine autumn and a wet winter. We lost in September for duty with the New Armies the permanent sergeant-instructors, one of whom had been attached to each company in peace time, but were fortunately allowed to retain our regular adjutant, Captain G. M. Sharpe, and the R.S.-M. (afterwards Lieut. Hanney, M.C.). About the close of the year the double-company system was adopted, under which the two headquarter companies became 'A' Company, under the command of Major Hedges, while Captain Battcock commanded B Company, composed of the men from Wallingford, Wantage and Newbury, Captain Lewis C Company, from Windsor and Maidenhead, and Captain Thorne D Company, from Abingdon and Wokingham. Many memories will remain with us of the laborious days and nights spent throughout those seven months, of company training in Highlands, fights on Galleywood Common, route marches up the long slope of Danbury Hill, journeys to Boreham Range in the darkness of a winter dawn, returning after dusk with a day's firing behind, and long hours spent in guarding the Marconi station in rain, snow and mist. All ranks were very keen and eager, especially before illness, the monotony of routine and disappointment at receiving no orders for overseas, produced some inevitable reaction. Colonel Serocold has indeed expressed his opinion that the battalion, while under his command, was never better trained than at the end of November, 1914.

At last, however, on the evening of March 30th, 1915,

amidst many expressions of goodwill and regret from the townsfolk, who thronged the streets, the battalion entrained for France, and left Folkestone in the S.E.R. packet boat *Onward* at 11 p.m.

CHAPTER 2

First Days on Active Service

The night was calm and bright with stars as, with an escorting destroyer, we crossed rapidly to Boulogne. After disembarking we marched to the Blue Base above the town, clattering over the cobbles, and drawing the heads of the curious to their bedroom windows. Here we lay down in tents and endured with the mitigation of one blanket a bitter frost. That evening we continued our journey towards the unknown from Pont des Briques station, where we found our train already contained the transport from Havre, two of whose number had been deposited on the line en route by the activities of a restive horse. The men were crowded into those forbidding trucks labelled *"Hommes, 40, chevaux, 8,"* and suffered much discomfort as the train crept through a frozen night, whose full moon illuminated a succession of dykes and water meadows stiff with hoarfrost, and bearded French Territorials with flaming braziers guarding the line. As dawn was breaking we detrained on the long platform of Cassel, and after the transport was unloaded moved up that steep hill which is so well known a landmark in Flanders. When we reached the summit, leaving the town on our left, we looked over the great Flemish plain, and heard for the first time the faint pulsing of the guns. The sun had now fully risen, and dissipated the thin morning mist;

the level country parcelled out into innumerable farms and clumps of trees stretched endlessly to the east. Only to the northward the steep outline of the Mont des Cats with the long ridge of the Mont Noir behind broke the plain. We descended, and made our way wearily to Winnezeele, a straggling village of outlying farms, close to the Belgian frontier. Here we remained three days, and with the zeal of new troops obeyed every letter of the law. Orderly sergeants descended into the village in marching order with full packs, no officer was ever seen without his revolver, while every billet was guarded as if at any moment it might be taken by assault.

On April 2nd we marched to Steenvoorde, where Lieut.-General Sir H. Smith-Dorrien, commanding 2nd Army, inspected the 145th Brigade. He congratulated them on their smart appearance, and spoke most warmly of the work already done by Territorials in the war. He also cheered us greatly by his anticipation of the fall of Budapest and of the forcing of the Dardanelles within the next few weeks.

On Easter Sunday, April 9th, we marched to Flêtre, a village on the great paved road to Lille, 3 miles short of Bailleul. Here long lines of lorries attested the importance of this main artery of the Army; while the effects of war were plainly seen in the bullet-riddled houses, the random little trenches and crosses dotted around, which recalled the successful fighting of the 4th Division on October 14th. The château which Headquarters occupied was said to have been similarly used for eight days by General von Kluck. Here for three days we enjoyed the rain of Flanders, and a foretaste of its eternal mud, before moving a stage nearer to the battle line, the flares of which had been an object of much interest at nights. Our next journey, on the 7th, led through Bailleul, where the band of the Artists' Rifles played in the great square, and the Warwicks of the 143rd Brigade viewed us with the superior air of men who had already been in the trenches with the 6th Division; then between the poplars along the Armentières road, until we turned to the left at Rabot, and soon arrived at our destination, a small village called Romarin. It lies just within the Belgian frontier, a bare 3 miles behind the firing line, whence the crackle of rifle fire was plainly audible, whilst from the coppiced slopes of Neuve Église, which bounded the northward view, intermittent flashes denoted the presence of the field batteries. The battalion was now attached to the 10th Brigade of the 4th Division, who were still holding the same ground where their victorious advance had come to a standstill in October in front of Ploegsteert Wood and northward round the base of Messines Hill. The four Companies were divided for their period of 48 hours in the line between 1st Warwicks, 2nd Seaforths, Royal Irish, Dublin Fusiliers, and 7th Argyll and Sutherland Highlanders (T.F.). The time passed without casualties or special incident, except for the shelling of a night working party under Lieut. Challoner, which escaped disaster only by good fortune. All will remember with gratitude the good comradeship and helpfulness of this Regular brigade, from whom we learnt much during our short period of attachment. On its conclusion we marched back to billets at Steenwerck, a station on the Lille line midway between Bailleul and Armentières. Here we endeavoured unsuccessfully, with the aid of a French officer, to locate a chain of signalling lamps impudently displayed from Bailleul right away towards the German lines.

On April 13th a Rugger match was played at Pont de Nieppe between teams representing the 4th and 48th Divisions, and resulted in a victory for the latter. Here Lieut. Ronald Poulton-Palmer, who captained the side, played his last game. On April 15th we moved up again, and took over for the first time our own line from the 2nd Hants at Le Gheer. The trenches ran here with singular angles and salients along the east face of Ploegsteert Wood; many disconnected posts, which could only be relieved by night, strong points in ruined houses with such suggestive names as First and Second German House were reminiscent rather of outposts than orthodox trench warfare. The weather was bright, the enemy entirely inactive, and the wood, with its oxlips and other spring flowers, its budding branches unscarred by shell fire, was a picture of charm rare in modern warfare. Forty-eight hours only were spent in this idyllic spot before we returned to Romarin to the accompaniment of the roar of mines, artillery, and concentrated rifle fire and machine gun fire, which heralded the sudden outbreak of the Battle of Hill 60, 4 miles to the north, just before sunset on April 17th. Our relief of the 4th Division was now complete, and our instructors marched to billets in Bailleul, only to be thrown within a few days into the furnace of the second Battle of Ypres. Before leaving they placed a great board just outside the Regent Street entrance to the wood, stating that it had been taken by the 4th Division on October, 1914, and handed over intact to us.

BERKSHIRE LINE AT PLOEGSTEERT

CHAPTER 3

Holding the Line at 'Plugstreet'

The line held by the Division for the next two months was wholly within Belgian territory, with a frontage of about 5,000 yards, which stretched from a point about 500 yards south-east of Wulverghem on the north to just below Le Gheer. The 143rd Brigade were on the left, 145th in the centre, and the 144th on the right. We were on the left of the 145th, and worked on a self-relieving system by which two Companies spent alternate periods of four days in the trenches and in local reserve. B and C Companies on the right shared trenches 37 and 38, also named Berkshire and Argyll; A and D in turn inhabited trenches 39 and 40, or Sutherland and Oxford, with a total frontage of 700 yards. The trenches ran along low ground between the wood and the River Douve; on the left the famous hill of Messines peered into our positions, and though itself barely 200 feet above sea-level loomed like a mountain among the mole-heaps of Flanders. The distance between the opposing lines varied from 450 to 250 yards. Reliefs could be carried out by day across the open on the right to Prowse Point (called after Major Prowse, of the Somerset L.I., who here organised a successful counter-attack in November, 1914, and afterwards was killed as a brigadier in the Somme battles); but the left was much in the air, as the only communication trench led up to some reserve breastworks near the Messines road, barely shoulder high, and themselves incapable of secure daylight approach, and all rations, stores, etc., had to be brought up overland by night over bullet-swept ground, but with negligible casualties.

The amenities of trench life depend almost wholly on the enemy and the weather. In both these respects we were fortunate. The Saxons who faced us lived up to their reputation, and apart from some accurate sniping which did more damage to periscopes than to human life, made no attempt to annoy us. No gas was ever emitted against us, though but a few miles to the north the enemy was using this new weapon incessantly. Throughout the end of April and for many days in May the wind blew steadily out of a cloudless sky from the north-east, and every morning we anxiously sniffed the breeze as we fingered the inadequate and clumsy respirators of those times. Every day a new pattern arrived with a new set of instructions. Then our sappers were ordered to make boxes of gun-powder which were to be fired by fuse and thrown over the parapet to dissipate the gas. In doing this they succeeded in blowing up several of their own number in their infernal den at Doo-Doo Farm. Scarcely, however, were these boxes ensconced in their weather-proof niches in each traverse than they were condemned, and the sweating infantry who had brought them up returned them with many curses to store.

The guns also left our sector in peace, which was the more fortunate as our artillery was not in a position to reply effectively to even a modest bombardment. Every now and then a little gun, apparently mounted on an armoured car which ran along the avenue just behind the German lines at dusk, would loose off half a dozen shells which burst without any warning, like a pair of gigantic hands clapping. Sometimes a few 'Little Willies' would strike Anton's Farm, which was included in our trench line, but no attempt was made to level this valuable ruin, which concealed patient and boastful snipers. The Warwicks on our left expiated the sins of the whole Division, and on most days it was possible to watch with a feeling of complete security a variety of shells bursting among them a few hundred yards away; while overhead flew the liberal daily ration expended on the Château de la Hutte on Hill 63 behind. From the lovely garden which surrounded it, luxuriant with lilac, Judas trees, tamarisk, wygelia and guelder-rose in full bloom, you could view, like Moses, the unapproachable land of promise, Lille and Roubaix, lying afar in the plain, with the smoke of enemy activity rising from their numerous tall chimneys.

We had our little excitements, as on May 9th, when the French attacked at Souchez, which was long remembered as 'the day of hate.' An elaborate demonstration was prepared by the brigade, of which the chief items were the exposure of trench-bridges 'obviously concealed,' and the firing throughout the day of long bursts of rapid fire. These interesting devices failed to deceive the enemy, who took little notice beyond shelling the unhappy Warwicks and the town of Ploegsteert with unusual severity. My company was in the wood that day in reserve, and lay about pretending to be in readiness. It was, in fact, the only day in which we had nothing to do.

We also had our mine, which was exploded opposite the Oxfords after two false starts with much pomp and ceremony. A green rocket was sent up one mile west of Ploegsteert 'to deceive the enemy,' as the Staff memorandum hopefully remarked. Captain Hadden, of the 1st/4th Oxfords, opposite whose trench the explosion was to occur, was ordered to keep half his company in the fire trench with the rifles and bayonets of the other half. These were to be ostentatiously waved above the parapet. The other half company spent some time marching up and down the corduroy paths in the wood, that the sound of their feet might suggest the arrival of large reinforcements. When the Brigade invited further suggestions of the same deceptive nature Hadden declared that he indented for magic mirrors *à la* Maskelyne and Devant, which would show the Oxfords not only in front but in rear of their enemy.

There was also the occasion when the gunners promised to destroy a new work erected by the Huns in front of their lines. They were heavily handicapped at the outset by the necessity of employing percussion shrapnel against a strong breastwork. But even when allowances were made, it seemed unnecessary that their first shell, a premature, should burst in the trees far behind on the Messines road, that the second should fall in our trenches, and the third damage our wire. The fourth, however, it is fair to say, reached if it did not seriously disturb its objective.

The ground between the lines offered many opportunities for patrolling; a belt of clover and rank weeds, knee-deep, in which our wire was enclosed, was succeeded by a deep watery ditch, also festooned with wire, and, beyond a fringe of willows on the further side, ran a wide field of rye able to conceal the tallest man. Each side cleared the ground immediately in front of their wire, and at nights the sickle of the enemy reaper could be plainly heard cutting swathes. More than once ambushes were laid in the daytime under cover of the rye, which waited for an opportunity against him till late at night, but without success. Lieut. Gathorne-Hardy, who was the pioneer of these daylight patrols, on one occasion, stayed out from noon till 4 p.m. with his faithful follower, Sergt. Westall, examining the German wire, for which exploit the former received the

M.C. and the latter the D.C.M. (to which was added a bar next year during the fighting at Pozières for devotion to the wounded). Our losses during these ten weeks were very light, but included Lieut. Ronald Poulton-Palmer, who was shot through the heart by a random bullet while superintending the building of a dugout just after midnight, May 4th, 1915. He had been nearly four years with the Battalion and was greatly beloved by all ranks; as I went down the line at stand-to that morning many of the men of old F Company, which he commanded at Chelmsford, were crying. He was the first officer to fall, and was buried by the Bishop of Pretoria in the Battalion cemetery in the wood on the east side of the Messines road, about 200 yards short of Hyde Park Corner.

The actual routine of life in the trenches was pleasant enough. The men knew exactly where they were. There was a time to eat, a time to sleep, a time for fatigues, and a time for sentry-go. There was little rain, and no bitter nights. The shelters, which held two or three men a-piece, though mere flimsy shell-traps, were comfortable, and either boarded or lined with straw, which was frequently renewed. When the Warwicks took over from us they exclaimed in admiring surprise, 'Why, they're all officers' dugouts.' Each section had its little oven made of a biscuit tin built round with clay. For the officers' mess in D Company we had the kitchen range from Anton's Farm, and a large zinc-covered erection in which six people could eat or play cards at once. The domestic element was supplied by two cats, who safely reared their offspring among us. Indeed, the calm of that placid series of days was such that it was difficult to realise that the second Battle of Ypres was raging with unbroken ferocity a few miles to the north, until we listened to the unwearied rumble of the guns and saw by night the great light in the sky where the doomed city blazed.

When in reserve our days were mainly spent in or close to the famous wood, which was at that time regarded as the show-place, *par excellence*, of the British front. Its natural glories have long since departed under the devastating shell fire of the latter days of the war, but in the spring and summer of 1915 it was a beautiful place, where one might fancy that the many British dead rested more easily beneath oaks and among familiar flowers than in most of the cemeteries of this dreary land. The wood was about 1-1/2 miles long, with a maximum depth of 1,400 yards, and its undergrowth, where not cut away, was densely intertwined with alder, hazel, ash, and blackthorn, with water standing in large pools on parts of its boggy surface. In one corner was the picturesque Fosse Labarre, a wide horseshoe moat enclosing a little garden, now a machine-gun emplacement, where grew the cumfrey, teazle and yellow flag. Everywhere the dog violet and blue veronica flourished in enormous clumps, and near the Strand was a great patch of Solomon's seal. It was a continual pleasure to see the wood clothe itself from the nakedness of early April and increase in fulness of life until we left at midsummer. The nightingale sang there unwearingly, but other birds were few, and I never noticed a nest in the wood. The few pheasants which survived a winter with the 4th Division were, I fear, exterminated by us. Rabbits continued plentiful in spite of rifles and snares, and every now and then a hare was started in the deserted fields.

Our predecessors had spent much labour and ingenuity in fitting up the wood for comfortable military habitation. It was everywhere intersected by corduroy paths, which though tiring to the feet, completely saved one from the horrors of the mud, and enabled rations and engineering stores to be brought up with ease in even the worst weather. Near the centre of the wood was Piccadilly Circus, whence many of these paths radiated; Regent Street and the Strand were the two great lateral highways; Bunhill Row preserved the memory of the London Rifle Brigade; Mud Lane served to remind us of those days when corduroy was still non-existent, whilst Spy Corner hinted at some grim and secret episode in the wood's history.

Meanwhile, screened from aeroplane observation by the dense foliage, the reserve Companies of the Brigade, lived in canvas tents fantastically daubed or in log huts. Some of the more elaborate of these latter served the double purpose of mess and bedroom for the Company Officers, the sides being taken up by two tiers of bunks made of wire and filled with straw. Outside the devices of the various regiments which had built or occupied them were carved or painted. Around them were little gardens, some of which with happy forethought had been planted in the winter. The most elaborate of all boasted a clump of Madonna lilies, and a red rose. We sowed vegetable seeds also, and ate our own mustard and cress, lettuces and radishes. In this connection, too, I should mention the 4,000 cabbages sent by Messrs. Sutton & Sons, which, planted in the transport lines at Rabot, were left for the consumption of the 5th Battalion when we moved south. These sylvan billets we generally shared with the 4th Oxfords, Hunterston North and South, peaceful spots, seldom visited by shells or stray bullets; less fortunate were the Bucks and 5th Gloucesters at Somerset House, further to the east. Here by night a steady drizzle of lead descended, and on one occasion 70 incendiary shells fell close to Headquarters. One of these was a dud, and the Bucks, determined to omit no precaution, sprinkled its resting place with chloride of lime! On the west side of the Messines road, just outside the wood, our Headquarters, with one reserve Company, inhabited the Piggeries, the enormous bricked and covered sties of which easily accommodated 200 men. The owner had only just completed his venture before war began, and the place was unmarked on the map, which possibly accounted for its immunity from shell fire.

Life in the wood would have been wholly pleasant but for two things, fatigues and lack of sleep. There is little doubt that if the war had gone on for fifty years, its last month would have found the men as strenuously employed in improving and strengthening the defences as in those early days. Soldiers are naturally inclined to think when depressed that (like the persons mentioned in the Bible) when 'they have done all that is required of them they are but unprofitable servants.' But at Plugstreet at least there was much which cried out urgently to be done. A great gap in the trench line just east of Prowse Point called for attention on our arrival. The work might, of course, have been highly dangerous, for it was carried on within 200 yards of the enemy. But no attempt was made to interfere with our labours. Presumably the mild Hun who faced us was afraid that he would be called upon to attack through the gap and rejoiced to see it filled. Every night the picks and shovels of 300 or 400 men could be heard merrily at work with the inevitable undercurrent of conversation as familiarity increased security. When the moon was bright the enemy could be seen peacefully attending to his own wire, while sometimes we were reminded that the hour had come to break off by a voice from opposite calling out, 'Time to pack up, sappers; go to bed.' Every morning a new length of enormous breastwork invited shells, which never came. On such occasions the thought arose that we must be taking part in the most expensive farce in the history of the world.

The lack of sleep was a more serious hardship, especially as it appeared avoidable. Owing, presumably, to the thinness with which the line was held, and to the lack of potential reinforcements behind, we were not allowed to sleep in the wood. Every night we made our way either to the lower or higher breastworks. The former were just off Mud Lane, and were consequently protected by the ridge from view, and to a certain extent from bullets. Here you could bivouac in the open under waterproof sheets, and except when the weather was very wet, enjoy a tolerable night. The latter, however, were on the forward slope, freely exposed to the continual fire with which the Huns replied to the provocation of the Warwicks. It was therefore necessary to lie at the bottom of a narrow and stinking trench on a 9-inch board. You had hardly fallen into an insecure doze when you were awakened and had to move out, for these breastworks, being barely shoulder high, were always evacuated at dawn, and dawn comes very early in June. The men naturally preferred the regular hours and the clean and comfortable shelters of the fire trench. Whenever any of the men desired to get rid of their pay quickly they had only to walk a few hundred yards to Ploegsteert village, where, within a mile of the firing line, some hundreds of the inhabitants still remaining sold bad beer, tinned fruit, and gaudy postcards at Flemish rates, which are the highest in the world. When shelling was severe they locked up their houses and disappeared mysteriously for a day or two until a renewed lull enabled them to restart their profitable shop-keeping. Many alleged spies lived here unharassed, especially in the outlying farms; and credibility was lent to the current tales by the number of carrier pigeons seen passing over the lines, or by the incident of the two dogs which suddenly appeared early one dawn from the German lines, leapt our trenches, and were lost in the darkness behind, in spite of Challoner's frenzied attempts to shoot them.

Besides its inhabitants Ploegsteert offered little of interest. The church, in spite of a dozen holes in the roof, and a great chip out of the east end, still reared its tall red-brick spire. On to the square outside the Huns directed a short afternoon hate at 3.30 punctually every day, reaching their target with wonderful precision, but doing little harm except when, as on May 9th, they employed incendiary shells. When baths and the disinfecting of trench-soiled clothing were required, the men marched to Nieppe, and wallowed in the famous vats, where Mr. Asquith, one day arriving unexpectedly, found himself cheered by a multitude of naked and steaming soldiers. From there it was but a short walk to Armentières, that centre of the great world, where Perrier water champagne and other delights could be obtained, where in a luxurious tea-room you were waited upon by female attendants of seductive aspect, and where two variety entertainments, the "Follies" and "Frivolities," were on view most nights. The ugly industrial town had then been little injured by shells, though every now and then it received its share. The Huns sometimes playfully directed against it French 220's captured at Maubeuge, and to point the witticism sent over a few duds inscribed '*Un Souvenir de Maubeuge.*'

So passed seven weeks during which we learned the routine of war under singularly favourable conditions.

CHAPTER 4

On the Move and
in Corps Reserve

During the first week in June the three Brigades left their own quarters and exchanged trench sections. The 145th moved from the centre to the left, to the joy of the Warwicks, whose losses had been considerable. While this move was in process the Battalion was taken out of the wood, and marched to huts at Korte Pyp, on a plateau with a wide prospect on the southern slopes of Neuve Église Hill. The site was admirable, the huts well-built and commodious, and (rarest of sights in the rich cultivation of Flanders) a good-sized grass field was at hand sufficiently level to make a decent cricket pitch. Here for four days we were free of fatigues, were inspected by the new G.O.C. of the Division, Major-General Fanshawe, enjoyed the sun, and endured a violent thunderstorm. Thence returning to the wood we sampled White Lodge, the Warwick's home under the steep wooded bluff of Hill 63, where the rats made merry among the dirt and unburied food; also La Plus Douce, a pastoral but dangerous spot, where the Douve flowed muddily amidst neglected water-meadows stretching along to Wulverghem with its battered church tower showing among the trees. On the opposite slope were two broken farms called St. Quentin and South Midland, wherein lay great quantities of abandoned tobacco, while all around were the tarnished scabbards thrown away by De Lisle's cavalry during the fighting at Messines of the previous October.

On June 15th the whole Battalion returned to the trenches, and held a total length of 1,450 yards, stretching from our old right, Trench 37, across the Messines road to a ruined cottage, close by which our trenches were carried over the Douve by a wooden bridge. Our line was thus drawn in a curve right round the south of Messines Hill, which twinkled with points of fire at every morning 'stand-to' from the tiers of trenches which honeycombed its face. Contrary to expectations, the centenary of Waterloo passed without incident during this tour, in spite of the Huns' reputed fondness for such celebrations.

At this time we were fortunate in having with us our 5th Battalion for instruction, who had come out about a fortnight before with the 12th Division, and there were many meetings of friends, both among the officers and the men.

We then returned for the last time to our familiar haunts in the wood, where we found the wild strawberries, which we had watched creeping timidly out of the earth, ripening everywhere in countless numbers. Meanwhile the 12th Division abode in billets in Armentières and Nieppe, and rumours grew strong that they would take over from us. The secret was well kept, but on Thursday morning, June 24th, as the Company Commanders were on their way to visit the Worcester trenches they were recalled by orderly with the news that the Battalion was moving to Bailleul that night. The evening was hot and steamy, the men soft from lack of exercise and sleep, and the 8 miles seemed interminable. We arrived at Bailleul about 1 a.m., and billeted in the quarter adjoining the railway station. For the first time since leaving England I slept in a bed with sheets in a room to myself.

A fierce thunderstorm next day had failed to clear the air, when we set out again about 9.30 p.m. in an atmosphere of clinging dampness. The whole brigade marched together with our faces turned south towards unfamiliar country, and just before daybreak we arrived at Vieux Berquin, a village of detached farmhouses with gardens full of all manner of fruit and vegetables. Here a dozen crosses with a smaller black cross painted on the wood testified to the presence of the Bavarians last autumn. That night, with the moon about the full, though often obscured by clouds, the brigade made a long and weary march south-west, edging gradually away from the flares and the distant rifle shots. Towards midnight we had a long check at Merville, a placid little town with tree-planted boulevards along the banks of the Lys, while Canadian guns and transport passed us going north from their second great fight at Festubert and Givenchy. Day had broken and the sun was climbing an eastern sky ribbed with red and gold, when we reached our destination, the village of Gonnehem, which boasts an ancient and beautiful church decorated with a quiet simplicity not often found in these parts. No enemy had entered here since the beginning of the war. It stands at the southern limit of the great plain; beyond are the low wooded hills of Artois, and away to the west the great slag heaps of Marles-les-Mines loomed through the thunder clouds like pyramids. That Sunday evening we completed our last stage of 4 miles by daylight, moving south-west again to the large industrial village of Lapugnoy, with a station on the St. Pol railway 5 miles west of Béthune, lying in a valley overlooked on either side by densely-timbered hills.

Here, withdrawn 10 miles behind the line and comfortably housed, we spent 17 days in a succession of drills, route marches and wood fighting. We were now in the 1st Army and behind the southern extremity of the then British line. From the calvary above the village the eye rested on many famous landmarks: the great cathedral of Béthune, untouched by the Hun, the church of Givenchy, the slag heaps of La Bassée, and the low ridge of Aubers, which barred the road to Lille, a dim frame in the background. We visited Béthune, a gracious little city girdled about with poplars, limes and chestnuts, where most things could be bought, including the latest English novels. The Guards had their Headquarters in the town, and impressed everyone with their physical fitness and splendid discipline. We consumed a morning waiting on the Lillers-Béthune road to see Lord Kitchener drive past in a motor; we watched the Indians going up to the trenches in motor 'buses, and a motley crew of picturesque French Colonials going by train to Souchez: Zouaves, turbaned and bearded, Algerians, with thick-lipped niggers from Congo and Senegal, who ran along the open trucks shouting and gesticulating. On July 11th a memorable meeting took place between the 1st and 4th Battalions in a field near Fouquières-lès-Béthune, where they spent the day together. This momentary gathering of so many brothers, relatives and friends on active service gave the greatest pleasure to all. In the improvised sports which ensued the men of the 1st Battalion beat the 4th at a tug-of-war, while in the officers' tug the result was reversed. The 1st Battalion were at this time commanded by Captain Bird, as their late C.O., Major Hill, had been killed not many days before by a shell which demolished the Headquarters' mess at Cuinchy.

The next evening found the brigade on the move again, through the mining villages of Marles-les-Mines and Bruay, to a wretched hamlet called Houchin, where the only accommodation provided for the battalion was a field of standing rye ripe for the scythe. When day broke we found ourselves in a desolate country with the high naked ridge of Notre Dame de Lorette shutting out the southern horizon. Here in shelter of boughs and waterproof sheets we spent three days of great discomfort under pouring rain and wind, employed day and night in digging a reserve line some 4 miles away. As we worked near Sailly-Labourse we gazed with curiosity at an arid gentle slope some 2 miles away, pitted by trenches and crowned by an elaborate iron structure with two towers. This ground was the scene of the main British attack on Loos two months later, and the building was the famous Tower Bridge. The squalid little town between Houchin and Sailly, at whose busy coal-mine the enemy intermittently threw shells, was Noeux-les-Mines, where Lord French had his forward headquarters during the fighting. But even then there was an abundance of the sound of battle, for on the second evening a furious cannonade burst out to the south-east, which signalled the recapture by the enemy of Souchez Cemetery: the last scene in that terrific fight which had endured almost incessantly since May 9th.

The day on which we went on the trek again (July 16th) was long remembered. We had expected in due course to go into the trenches somewhere near Grenay, but it suddenly became known that the brigade was to march back to the neighbourhood of Lillers preparatory to entraining for an unknown destination. Half the battalion that day had done their daily trip to Sailly and came back about 4 p.m., after marching 8 miles and digging for four hours. At 9 p.m. we moved off in driving rain for an all-night march of 15 miles. The brigade transport was in front, and checks were naturally frequent as we retraced our steps through Bruay and Marles, thence on to Burbure, where our guide misled us through a narrow inky lane, in which most of the Brigade lost touch. Just as the dawn was breaking and our troubles seemed nearly over our guide again mistook the way, and we found ourselves bogged in a cart track at the top of a down. The rain and hail descended in a sudden most violent squall and wetted us to the skin; while far away in the east the morning flares twinkled for 30 miles in a great arc. One of the signallers was heard plaintively to remark as we waited, 'What 'ave we done to deserve all this?' Finally we descended into Lières, a pleasant remote village in a fold of the chalk, full of cherry trees, and slept peaceably till noon.

After a day's rest we marched on Sunday afternoon, July 18th, to La Berguette station, on the Hazebrouck line west of Lillers. Here we met detachments of our old friends of the wood, the L.R.B., who, reduced in strength to 70 men during the Ypres fighting, had been put on lines of communication. We knew by now that our journey would take us to Doullens, a sub-prefecture of the Somme, and that we were to take over a portion of the French line. So back again in the cattle trucks and second-class carriages, the Battalion moved off south under far more pleasant circumstances. The rate of speed, too, was comparatively high and can hardly have fallen short of 15 miles an hour.

We reached our destination as usual in the early hours of the morning, and after unloading drew out of the town, passing on the right the old Citadelle with its red ramparts high upon a hill, and the point of elderly Territorials at the junction of the great Amiens road. Thence we followed the south bank of the Authie River, enclosed on either side by rounded chalk hills 400 or 500 feet high. We breakfasted by the road opposite the Château of Autheuille, where Major Barron and his M.T. lived luxuriously for many months 11 miles behind the firing line; then plodded on past Sarton, where the 5th Gloucesters watched us from their billets, and finally bivouacked in the beech woods of Marieux. Close by was the site of the French aerodrome, now deserted save for empty petrol tins; down in the valley, Mon Plaisir, an enormous country house was being prepared for the Headquarters of the 7th Corps; in the orchards were parked two batteries of long French 155's. The roads were encumbered with the impedimenta of two armies. We were starting on another stage of the great adventure, and felt again to a lesser degree the uncertainty of essaying the unknown.

CHAPTER 5

Relieving the French
at Hébuterne

After 36 hours in the wood we packed up again and moved by night through Authie, afterwards most familiar and welcome of rest billets, passing Coignieux, where the French gunners, sitting by their fires in the horse lines, called out greetings, and ascended the northern hill to Bayencourt, a stinking little village full of flies and odours.

By now the enemy had apparently got wind of the coming of the English (which was first confirmed, according to prisoners, by the discovery of English bullets fired at their trenches), for during the next few days aeroplanes flew constantly over the village at a great height. In a field close by a French 75, which moved with a circular traverse round a platform of greased wood let into a small pit, endeavoured to arrest their progress with a wonderfully rapid barrage, and to throw them back into the area covered by the next gun. Its adjutant had spent several years in a solicitor's office at Ealing, and spoke excellent English.

Our ultimate destination was now the sector of Hébuterne, which had leapt into prominence on the occasion of the successful French attack on Touvent Farm, June 12th, but was now, from all accounts, peaceful enough. The 5th Gloucesters and 4th Oxfords were the two first to go into the trenches, where the French received them with enthusiasm, putting fresh flowers in all the dugouts, and writing up everywhere greetings of welcome.

My brother (Captain G. H. W. Cruttwell) went before us into Hébuterne with part of B Company to relieve the guards of the 93rd Regiment posted round the village, a ceremony more interesting and impressive than the relief of the trenches by reason of its greater formality. He dined with their officers afterwards, and was presented, as a farewell gift, with the best mattress in the village. The rest of the battalion started after sunset on July 22nd, passing a battalion of Frenchmen returning by half platoons from the trenches, and marched into Hébuterne, a most interesting example of the ruined village organised for defence, situated 600 yards only behind the front line trenches. It was destined to be our forward billet for many months, and to become as familiar to us in the smallest details as our own homes. A somewhat detailed description will therefore perhaps not be without interest.

Hébuterne was a good-sized village of about 1,000 inhabitants, on no highway but the converging point of many small roads, lying in a very slight pocket of the rolling chalk plateaux of Artois, surrounded on every side by the orchards of the local bitter cider apple, with a village green in the centre, and a pond surrounded by tall poplars. The length of the village was about 900 yards, and its average breadth about 500 yards. Almost every house was a one-storied farm of three to four rooms, with considerable outbuildings of mud and plaster, capable of accommodating in close billets one or two platoons. There were no large houses, the so-called château on the Bucquoy road being a very moderate mansion, and, apart from it, the rectory, mairie, the mill by the pond used as Brigade Headquarters, and the pleasant villa called Poste Cambronne, alone stood out in modest prominence. There were very few inns, the largest of which bore the touching and appropriate sign, 'A la Renaissance.'

At the south end of the village stood the church, a broken gaping shell of red brick with imitation marble pillars; it was afterwards razed to the ground by the sappers, who required its bricks and perhaps thought it too good a range-mark to exist so near their store.

When we arrived we found, to our surprise, two civil inhabitants clinging to their ruinous homes; one who held some vague post of authority called himself a Garde Champêtre; another, an aged crone, suddenly emerged cursing from her hovel to expostulate with me for unwittingly stealing her peas and young carrots. They were cleared out immediately after our arrival. The flight of the remainder had been evidently precipitate. Not only had beds, tables, and all bulkier pieces of furniture been abandoned, but knives, forks, crockery and many little china ornaments. The village had been reoccupied after a stubborn fight in October, 1914, and the enemy pushed well beyond its uttermost limits. In the western orchards was the large French cemetery, and hard by that of our own division, adjoining a cricket pitch, where we had many spirited games of tip and run.

Though naturally much broken up, with perhaps a dozen houses left intact, the village had never been so populous in days of peace. Not less then 3,000 troops lived there above or below ground, including the brigadier and at least three battalion commanders. That portion of the village which lies north of the pond had been made into a fortified redoubt known as the Keep, the garrison of which was the equivalent of one battalion, whose O.C. lived in the Poste Cambronne, a much desired residence until an 8.2 shell demolished its upper story in December. Very few shells indeed ever fell in the Keep until the beginning of 1916, the chief targets being the pond and the area round the church. The village was fortunate in being practically screened from direct observation by a slight rise in ground between it and the enemy, and the indirect machine gun fire which raked the streets at odd intervals was curiously ineffective, for the majority of shots went high, though on occasions one had to abandon respect and lie flat in the mud, until the shower was overpast.

We sampled all corners of the village—the Serre Cross Roads, where the rain came through the roof and the machine gun bullets through the wall of our crazy billet; the château, with its broken conservatory, its fig tree, Christmas roses, and what we believed to be the only arm-chair in Northern France; 'D' Farm, where Private Meads, our first casualty in the village, was killed by a 4.2-inch just outside the window; and 'B' Farm, with its collection of plates and ornaments amassed on the first morning before most of the village was out of bed. Battalion Headquarters were first in the house on the Mailly-Maillet road, afterwards appropriated by the Brigade, who hollowed out for themselves great caverns in the earth: then in the little house by Serre Cross Roads, where the owners had chalked up an appeal to the French to take care of their newly-weaned calf; and finally in the factory by the pond, where shells through Q.M. Payne's bedroom and the gate posts drove them, too, underground, and led to the erection of an enormous bulwark of sandbags 15 feet high, to protect the mess.

The defences of the village were formidable, and when one got to know them, simple, in spite of the bewilderment caused by a first inspection of what appeared to be a mere labyrinth. The Keep, as has been mentioned, was simply a redoubt with trenches facing all points of the compass, its

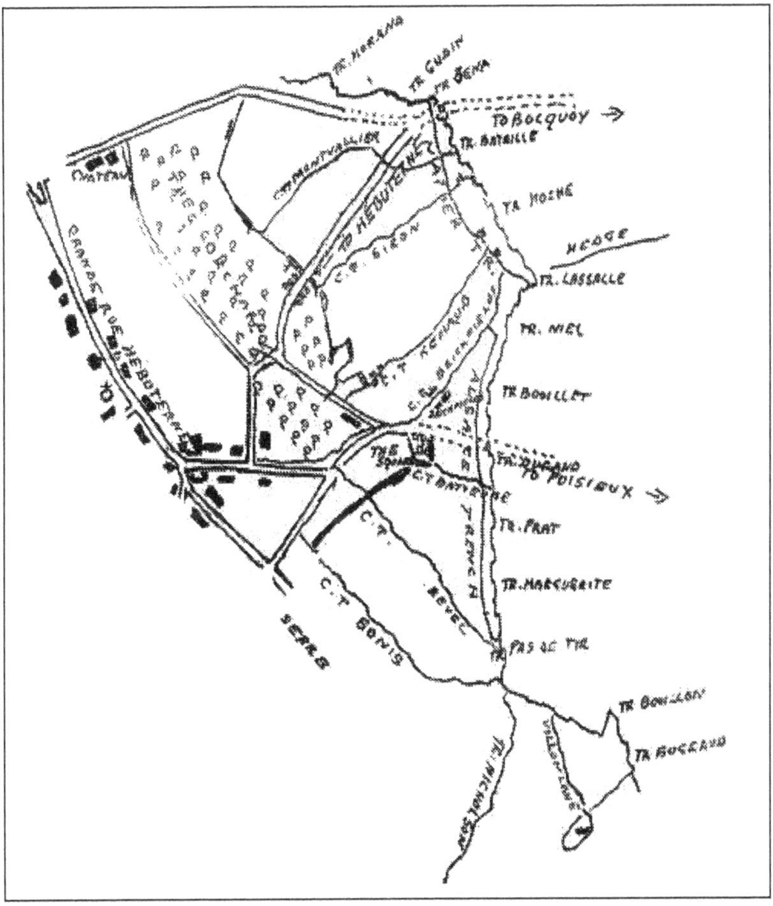

TO BOCQUOY
TR. BATAILLE
TR. MOINE
HEDGE
TR. LASSALLE
TR. NIEL
TO PUISIEUX
TR. PRAT
TR. MARGUERITE
PAS DE TIR
CHATEAU
ORCHARD
TO HEBUTERNE
C.T. GIRON
THE SQUARE
C.T. BONIS
SERRE

two points of chief tactical importance being the Mound, eminently suited for enfilade machine gun fire, and the barricades which closed the Keep to any enemy already in possession of the village to the south of the pond. It will be seen, by studying the map, that the whole of the eastern face of Hébuterne was protected by two lines of defences, outer and inner. The former were 200 to 300 yards beyond the edge of the houses, and were excellently sited along a hedge for almost the whole of their length. They were connected with the first line fire trench by communication trenches about every 100 yards. The inner defence, running through the orchards, just covered the village, and was connected both with the outer line and with the cellars of the houses by numerous communication trenches. Finally the western exits of the village were commanded by a group of trenches astride the Sailly road on rising ground. All this scheme had been completed by the French before our arrival, and reflected great credit on both their tactical skill and the energy required in construction.

When we turned from the village to the trenches we found also many points of interest and contrast. In Artois, unlike Flanders, you can dig to your heart's content, or, to speak more accurately, you can get a surfeit of digging. The soil is either a light manageable clay, or more frequently chalk. Here, then, we met with none of the conspicuous breastworks of our old home, but fire trenches more than 6 feet deep, and communicators whose bottoms were 8 or 9 feet below ground level. Many of the dugouts, moreover, were elaborate caves, large enough to accommodate 25 men, and capable, with their roofs of logs heaped over with many feet of earth, of resisting the direct impact of a 5.9-inch shell. The increase in security was naturally great, and bombardments which would have destroyed whole trench sections at Ploegsteert were almost ineffective. In the winter, however, under stress of rain and snow, the dugouts fell in, together with the sides of the trench, which, from lack of material, could not be efficiently revetted. Then men sighed for Trench 40, and the little sandbag shelters too small to collect such quantities of water. But as we viewed them then the dugouts seemed the last word in luxury; one of those which I inhabited contained a mattress, two chairs, a table, a large gilt-framed mirror, some artificial flowers, a portrait of the Czar and his wife, and an engraving called 'Le Repos du Marin,' which depicted an old sailor drinking peacefully under a tree. All would have been well but for the small game; lice, a legacy from the French, enormous red slugs, which ate any food which lay about, and left a viscous trail behind every movement, countless swarms of mice and gigantic rats, some of which were so bold as to gnaw through the men's haversacks, as they slept, in search of the food contained therein.

We naturally examined every detail of these new trenches with minute interest, and compared English and French models. The first sensation was of bewilderment. For at Ploegsteert we had been content with a very simple system; wayfaring men, though fools, could scarcely err therein. But here we had to learn our way about a perfect maze of trench, where it was easy, or rather inevitable, at first to go wrong, and, finding yourself enclosed by earth walls towering above your head, to lose all sense of direction. This difficulty was not lessened for the men by our retention of all the French names for the trenches, most of which were christened after their Generals. Such names as Bugeaud, Poniatowski, Bataille, and the like, were so many pieces of gibberish which it was hardly possible for a self-respecting English soldier to pronounce, while Boyau, Abri, Feuillée and Puisard were not helpful forms of iden-tification. But anyone who had become familiar with the labyrinth would at once admit that for purposes of relief and inter-communication it was far superior to anything he had yet seen.

Another useful novelty was the systematic use of saps for night-posts. A sentry in the fire trench will always find his attention distracted to a certain degree, especially when he is 500 yards from the enemy, but put him in a sap-head with only a few yards of wire to protect him, and the acuteness of his vision and hearing will be marvellously increased.

On the other hand, in certain points the French trenches fell below the standards to which we had accustomed ourselves. Owing to their superiority in artillery, and to the thinness with which they held their front line, they did not bother to build strong traverses between the inordinately long fire bays, which were, in consequence, seriously exposed to oblique gun fire. Again, no attempt had been made to provide any flooring for the trenches, and the Battalion spent many happy hours working under the August sun as amateur bricklayers, with the material ready to hand from the village, in the hope, which the winter was to bring utterly to naught, of thereby providing a solid bottom.

Chapter 6

Summer and Autumn in Artois

During the six weeks after our arrival the weather was very broken, with many violent thunderstorms and very little heat. Except for eight days at Sailly, where fear of aeroplanes was fortunately sufficient to prevent parades, but not cricket in the orchards, we spent all our time at Hébuterne. The Battalion, for the most part, relieved itself as at Plugstreet, but had no fixed dwelling-place, sometimes extending as far to the right as Trench Bugeaud, half way up the north slope of the hill of Serre, where the ground was littered with the debris and decomposing bodies of the June fighting, sometimes as far to the left as Trench Morand, about 300 yards north of where the Bucquoy road crossed the trenches. From Morand to Hoche the lie of the land was all in our favour; the trenches were sited just in front of the gentle rise which covered Hébuterne; 500 to 600 yards away, at the bottom of the dip lay the enemy, about 40 feet below us, and behind him the ground again rose leisurely and showed its slope towards us for 3,000 yards, with the hand of the Hun writ large in chalk, revealing his second and third line with the great covered communication trenches which connected them. The left of the picture was closed by Gommecourt Wood, of sinister memory, with its pretty little red-roofed village encased therein, and its gaping cemetery sticking out from the south-east corner. On the skyline appeared several battered farms, La Brayelle, Les Essarts, and Rettemoy, each surrounded by copses and orchards, and on their right the Bois de Biez, which provided a home for those thorns in our flesh, the 5.9-inch howitzers. On its right flank again running down the hill towards us was the Bois Rossignol, where an active battery of field guns made music less tuneful than that of the bird whence the wood was named.

Straight in front of Trench Bataille, about 900 yards away, stood the skeleton of the little farm called by the French Sans Nom. It was the favourite point on which every type of gun registered, and the Germans attached great importance to its bowels, for night after night hand-carts unloaded there, and men could be heard by patrols talking and hammering. Much interest and amusement could be obtained from this panorama with field glasses and telescope. Along the road which ran obliquely from Les Essarts to Gommecourt came cyclists, fatigue men, and occasionally formed bodies of troops, who, when assailed with long range machine gun fire, extended and advanced in short rushes. One day two fat Huns carrying a dixie walked along the side of the great chalk communication trench, who, when Sergeant Daniels fired a shot at 1,200 yards, dropped their burden and leapt nimbly into the trench. One morning when Goolden and I were looking through a telescope we noticed a trestle table being put up near Rettemoy Farm: this was followed by half a dozen German officers accompanied by two ladies dressed in white, who, after surveying the view, sat down to lunch. We thought this too good an opportunity to miss, and informed the F.O.O. By describing this little gathering as a working party, he obtained the major's permission to fire, and the ladies' meal was soon interrupted by four rounds of shrapnel.

Opposite Lassalle a shoulder ran out towards the German lines with its steep northern face covered with dense thickets of thorn, apt cover for night adventures; this shoulder so restricted our view that from one trench the field of fire amounted to no more than 10 yards. If you walked south you passed the Puisieux road, opposite which and some 500 yards away was a clump of tall poplars between the lines generally known as the Seven Sisters. There was a superstition that this was held by the enemy, but when explored by a daylight patrol of the 5th Gloucesters nothing was discovered in the nature of defences. South of the road the line curved south-west into lower ground and became separated from the opposing trench by 900 yards. From here another wide prospect unfolded itself, with Puisieux 2 miles away, lifting its white spire from a knoll enclosed on three sides by beech woods. Behind an occasional wisp of smoke showed that a train was making its way between Achiet and Miraumont, whose supply depots were frequently visited by our bombarding squadrons. A mile to the south the hamlet of Serre, twice fruitlessly attacked next year, topped a barren and shell-blown ridge. About this point, notorious for frequent visits from the earth-shelling aerial torpedo, began the lines of the 4th Division, once again our neighbours. They were our sister division in the 7th Corps, which was completed by the arrival at the end of August of the 37th Division, who after spending some days with us for instruction relieved the French on our left at Fonquevillers and Hannescamps. The commander of the 3rd Army, which was gradually increased until its line extended to the southern marshes of the Somme, was at this time Sir C. Monro, afterwards Commander-in-chief in India.

The month of August passed quietly with us, though rendered notable by the great German successes in Russia.

The fate of Warsaw moved the enemy to put up notice-boards announcing the event, one of which had on one side 'Warschau Gefallen,' and on the other, apparently reversable by a string, 'Gott Strafe England.' With commendable caution, however, they were planted so near their own trench that it required a field glass to read them. A few days later, when the German Fleet met with misfortune in the Gulf of Riga, Sergt. Tester posted a board with details of that reverse just in front of their barbed wire. The French batteries remained with us for a month, while our gunners were registering, and given a free hand in accordance with the British custom of annoying the enemy incessantly, showed a complete mastery over him.

Throughout the night at uncertain intervals their guns threw shells into Gommecourt. It was difficult to believe that the terrible explosions which resulted were caused by a shell lighter than our 18 pounders, whose shrapnel burst with an almost inaudible 'pip.' Practically the only retaliation indulged in by the Germans was to shell our batteries as they were getting into their gun-pits, though without serious damage. About the end of the month, however, a serious misfortune befell A Company, one of whose platoons was half destroyed by a 4.2-inch, which struck the Brickfields, a dangerous and conspicuous supporting point. The men had just returned from bathing in the village, when the shell fell among them, killing five and wounding nine. At the same spot also Lance-Corpl. Boston, of B Company, was blown to pieces while gallantly remaining out to see that the working party under his charge had taken cover safely.

On September 3rd, Captain (now Major, O.B.E.) Porter, Secretary of the County Association, spent a night with the Battalion in the trenches, and was thus able to assure the people of Berkshire, if such assurance was needed, that its Territorial Battalion was doing its fair share of the laborious task of holding the British front line. Next day, after a month's continuous residence in Hébuterne or the trenches, we were relieved by the 144th Brigade. The relief was carried out in daylight, both Brigades marching boldly along the Sailly road, the crest of which was in clear distant view of the enemy. The two intermediate communication trenches, Larrey and Jena, some 2,500 yards long, were not yet sufficiently repaired for our passage. This labour of love was accomplished by the 5th Sussex, who were attached to the Brigade as Pioneer Battalion, and lived at Sailly. We marched to Authie, 7 miles back, and remained there 12 days; this village was until January to be the rest billets of ourselves and the 4th Gloucesters for alternate periods. It lies in the valley of the Authie River, between downs of chalk, beech-covered, which put on beautiful colours as soon as the first frosts of autumn touched them. The whole countryside is indeed strangely reminiscent of the Chiltern Hills of Oxfordshire and Bucks. Battalion Headquarters were at the Château, a substantially-built, comfortable house under the southern slopes of the hills, belonging to a widow, Madame De Wailly, who lived there with her two daughters. Most of the best billets were occupied by the elderly heroes of the A.O.D. and the Ammunition Column, but it is a roomy village, and accommodated us without difficulty. The measure of its prosperity may be gauged by the fact that whereas before the war there were three shops, there were now 27. Our principal work was to make thousands of hurdles in the Bois de Warnimont, which greatly to the men's disgust mysteriously disappeared as soon as made; for when we indented for them in the trenches we received no more than 17 for the whole Brigade. Presumably they went to beautify the corps line, which was such a model of perfected trench artistry that it seemed almost a pity that it was never likely to be used. In this wood in company with a few fallow deer, a Navvies' Battalion lived under canvas, who performed most useful work in digging flints and repairing the roads. In age they ranged from 40 to 70, and were a cheery crew, mainly from Wales. Their notions of military discipline were, as may be imagined, singular, and it is credibly reported that on one occasion, when General Fanshawe rebuked a navvy for not saluting him, the offender beckoned with his thumb towards a pal and exclaimed, "'Ere, Bill, come and 'ave a look at this.'

On September 7th General Monro, G.O.C. 3rd Army, inspected the Battalion, who were drawn up in old quarter-column formation with 12 paces interval in the Berkshire field on the west outskirts of the village. He was greatly pleased with the appearance of the Battalion, and in his subsequent address thus expressed his satisfaction:

'After hearing what your Divisional General has said of you, I expected to see a very fine body of men on parade to-day, and I can assure you—I say so straight out—that I am not in the very least disappointed. Your bearing as well as your order and steadiness in the ranks, and the way in which you put your equipment on, all go to show that you know the right thing, and prove the high standard which you set before you. I am well acquainted with your 1st Battalion, and have served with them in this present war. They have lived up to the high traditions which attach to the regiment, and to the good name which they have won in the past. You are proud to belong to such a regiment; you have already reached a high standard, and I hope and believe you will continue to retain that high standard.... I hear from your Divisional Commander that you have con-scientiously carried out all the work allotted to you. In the sentry line your vigilance has been beyond all criticism. You have done good work in all that pertains to the work of the trenches, digging and so on. Moreover, your conduct in the village and in billets has been uniformly good.'

During this stay at Authie rumours began to be active. It was persistently reported that the 'great offensive' would be in full swing before September was out. Some of the A.S.C., who had been buying coal at Marles-les-Mines, reported that the country round Béthune was incredibly thick with guns, while a similar and more detailed forecast was brought back by officers who had dined with the 4th Divisional Headquarters. Then leave, which had been on more or less regularly since the beginning of June, was indefinitely stopped. Thus, though no one yet knew the date arranged for the opening of the battle, expectations were abroad, and each morning the significance of any unusual cannonade was eagerly discussed. Amidst such an atmosphere of uncertainty we relieved the 4th Gloucesters at Hébuterne on September 17th, making the passage from Sailly over the brow of the hill for the first time by the congested Boyau Larrey.

For a few days we lived our ordinary trench life, and helped to instruct a company of the 13th Manchesters; but on September 21st the bombardment from the sea to the Vosges opened in our sector, with short fierce bursts of fire on the enemy villages and roads. On September 23rd, at 7.30 a.m., a squadron of 21 aeroplanes, spread loosely over the sky, flew over Hébuterne to attack the station of Valenciennes; throughout this day the roar of the guns to north and south was continuous; as the sun set a fierce thunderstorm came up, and the rival rumblings and flashes of nature and machinery in the dusk made a sufficiently lurid prelude for battle. On the 24th it became generally known that in certain contingent events, carefully kept secret, the Brigade would attack between Gommecourt Wood and the Puisieux road, with the Berks and the Bucks in the leading waves. Accordingly, the gunners got to work, and the 18-pounders cut three narrow lanes in the enemy wire (which each night the patient Hun carefully repaired), while the howitzers played on the forts and beehive structures in Gommecourt Wood and near Ferme Sans Nom. It was far and away their biggest show up to date, but the number of rounds fired by the Divisional Artillery in the three hottest days was only 5,000, an amount which, by present-day standards, appears ludicrously small. Meanwhile, two platoons of 5th Sussex, cursing the fortune which had brought them up again to the trenches, were packed into the battalion sector to look after our belongings, if we went over.

Saturday, the 25th, broke wet and misty; the lovely autumn weather of the past fortnight had gone for good. The gunners were unable clearly to see their targets, or to mark by the spurt of dry earth the exact strike of their wire-cutting shrapnel. Through the mist on that most inappropriate morning appeared a herd of cows and men harvesting between Rossignol and Puisieux, not much more than a mile from our lines.

During the day a notable series of messages came through from G.H.Q., and it seemed at first as if the attack had broken the German lines, as we identified on our maps those names then unfamiliar—Loos, Hill 70, Hulluch, Cité St. Elie, and Cité St. Auguste—which successive messages announced as having passed into our hands. Then came the reports from Champagne with their impressive and ever-growing lists of guns and prisoners. The men were in high spirits, and some of B Company were heard making bets as to who would take the first German prisoner. Towards evening, however, the messages spoke only of violent counter-attacks and ground lost, while it was announced that the attack of the French Corps on our immediate left had failed completely. When this message reached Major

50

Hedges in the Keep just as he was turning in, he summed up our general feeling by his remark: 'Well, I think I can take my boots off now.' Throughout the whole of Sunday expectation was at its highest pitch, for all believed that if the general advance was coming it would come quickly. But there was little positive news beyond the short French statement: 'We have taken Souchez.' Yet in the evening all the last preparations for attack were hastily carried through. A Berks and a Bucks dump were dug in the trenches, in which were collected all the engineering material required for an assault—tools, sandbags, trench bridges and flags for marking out positions in the captured line. The Brigade Signallers were busy putting up directions everywhere for the Bucks, who were to take over the left of our line: and new maps were issued to come into use at midnight. The night was very disturbed with bursts of rapid fire, and once a great cheer from the Warwicks at Fonquevillers, who were simulating an attack; while thousands of spent bullets from the 37th Division in the loop north of Gommecourt came wearily to rest in our trenches, several of which struck sentries in the sap-heads without doing them any harm. Early next morning a British aeroplane flew very low over the enemy trenches and, as desired, drew heavy fire, thereby proving them to be full of men, a matter in doubt before, as they had not responded to our attempts at provocation. But during the day it became increasingly clear that the great scheme had failed; for, although a message came from 3rd Army saying 'that in view of the great Allied successes both north and south it is possible that the Germans may evacuate their trenches, and in that case you must be prepared to slip quietly into them at a moment's notice,' its effect was more than discounted by a simple message which read: 'Work may now be resumed as usual in the trenches.' The enemy, meanwhile, appeared to be well acquainted with our plans, for voices were heard calling out, 'Come on, Bucks, come on, Berks!' 'The Royal Berks will lead the attack,' while a humorist shouted from the fort at Gommecourt, 'Run away, English; go away home.' The enemy had indeed good reason to be confident in the strength of these positions, which twice next year were to defy capture after the most elaborate preparation. The turmoil of the last few days was now succeeded by a complete calm in which scarcely a gun spoke.

On September 30th we were relieved in due course by the 6th Gloucesters, but went not to Authie, which was considered too far away, but to Souastre, a village in the area of the 37th Division, five kilometres west of Fonquevillers. As we approached we were played into the village by our band of drums and fifes, which had just arrived from England. Here the Battalion remained for six days in readiness to move at half an hour's notice, with baggage and transport reduced to a minimum, before we returned to Authie and resumed for many months to come our customary alternation of trench duty and rest, though the respective periods were in future lessened from 12 days to 8.

By our next return to the trenches autumn was already merging into early winter in this chilly tableland, with sharp night frosts and thick white mists. For days on end it was almost impossible to distinguish the hostile lines: and so the guns maintained their silence, for it was unprofitable to fire where you could not observe, and our own people had the strictest orders to economise rigorously until the expenditure of the Loos battles had been again made good. Such weather gave the finest opportunity for patrols, whose wanderings were made easier by the apparent indifference of the enemy. His saps and barbed wire were examined more than once, but though hares were started constantly in the thick tangled grass, only once were his patrols encountered. On this occasion a party of ten, moving in a dense fog and pitch darkness along the enemy wire, was challenged, and a lively fight ensued for a few minutes with rifles, revolvers and bombs, in the course of which Private A. Gibbs, of D Company, a huge, stout-hearted soldier, specially distinguished himself. As generally happens in these blind affrays, there was more noise than damage, and our patrol, which was considerably outnumbered, made its way safely back. One man who became separated from his comrades remained, uncertain of his direction, in No Man's Land for eight hours, until sunrise showed him his bearings. An officer and sergeant of the 10th Royal Irish Rifles, who formed part of the patrol, were spending their first tour of instruction with us in the trenches.

On October 17th-18th the general calm was rudely broken by the performance of the Bavarian Circus, a travelling siege train of 5.9's with a few heavier pieces, which retaliated effectively from the Bois de Biez for our September bombardments. The first day's firing was directed on the forward billets, Hébuterne, Sailly and Colincamps, with short fierce bursts from six or seven batteries firing simultaneously. Next day it was the turn of the Trenches. On the left of the battalion sector part of D Company held a little salient position which enclosed a thicket standing steeply some 12 feet above the Bucquoy road. The enemy apparently believed it to be used for observation purposes, and frequently directed fire upon it, but in point of fact it was untenanted by day. On this salient and on its approaches, a total trench line of about 150 yards, the Bavarians threw during an hour about 400 5.9's, not to mention smaller shells, while two field guns galloped into Gommecourt Park and unlimbering in full view fired obliquely at the wire from point-blank range. They were harassed and eventually forced to retire by the action of Lieut.

Coombes, of the Bucks, on our left, who gallantly got a machine gun into the open and took them in the flank. Our own guns were not available at the time, as they were themselves engaged in a 'shoot' and busy on pre-arranged targets. Although the trenches were cut to pieces and the thicket levelled by the fire, which was of extreme accuracy, not a single serious casualty was incurred. Captain Thorne had his Company Headquarters just behind the salient, and his dugout received several hits, and bulged ominously, but did not give way. All wires were cut, but were promptly repaired by the Company Signallers in the heat of the bombardment. Meanwhile, the Oxfords had been assailed with much greater violence, and over 2,000 shells fell in their lines; while their communication trenches were barraged with lachrymatory shells. It almost seemed as if an infantry attack might be imminent, and colour was lent to this theory by an aeroplane message saying that what appeared to be gas cylinders were observed along the enemy trenches between Gommecourt and Serre. Accordingly we stood-to all night repairing the shattered trenches and re-erecting the wire. The hostile infantry who probably disapproved of their artillery's activity as likely to bring future trouble upon themselves, made no attempt to hinder with rifle or machine-gun fire our all-night task. This was by far the heaviest and most concentrated bombardment which the Battalion had yet sustained.

CHAPTER 7

Winter in the Trenches

In spite of many rumours of a rest the 48th Division remained in the line throughout the whole of the winter, and, indeed, as we shall see, until the spring of 1916 was far spent. Meanwhile, the wastage of the Battalion was considerable, and was not made good by drafts, whose total number up to March 1st, 1916, amounted only to 103 men. Companies, therefore, with a fighting strength of from 90 to 110 men had to hold (under far more trying conditions) the same frontage (about 1,400 yards as a rule) which had been allotted to them when at practically full strength in the summer. It is true that a company of some New Army battalion was constantly arriving for instruction, but during the two or three days of their visit they could not relieve our men of any of the burden. On the contrary, the work and responsibility, especially for officers and N.C.O.'s was considerably increased, and the difficulty of finding accommodation in the teeming hive of Hébuterne for an extra 250 men added to the general discomfort. A certain amount of change, however, from trench routine was afforded by the courses now established at the various schools of instruction behind the line; for instance, one officer and 30 men went every fortnight to the Brigade Bomb School at

Sailly, and in spite of constant shelling found reasonably comfortable billets.

Although casualties still, happily, remained light, and no officer had been killed since Lieut. Poulton-Palmer, considerable changes took place during the winter which it is convenient to summarise here. Colonel Serocold left the Battalion on February 14th, 1916. He had served with the regiment for 32 years, and had commanded it for 11-1/2. All Berkshire people know of the affection and respect with which he was regarded by the regiment, which alone can fully appreciate the debt they owe to his training and personal example. He was succeeded by Major (now Lieut.-Colonel) R. J. Clarke, C.M.G., D.S.O. The adjutant, Captain G. M. Sharpe, had already left in the previous October, and was afterwards to command his first Battalion. In losing him we all felt that we were losing not only an ideal adjutant, but a personal friend. He was succeeded by Lieut. L. E. Ridley, who was killed next August, near Pozières. The two commanders of A and D Companies, Major F. R. Hedges and Captain H. U. H. Thorne, came home through sickness about the end of 1915. Captain Thorne afterwards won distinction in command of the 12th Royal Scots, and was killed in the Battle of Arras, April 9th, 1917, leading the first wave of assault 'in the old chivalrous way,' as his Brigadier wrote. Captains W. E. M. Blandy and R. G. Attride assumed command of A and D Companies respectively. R.S.-M. Hanney also left, to our great regret, and received a commission in the 1st Battalion, where he afterwards won an M.C. His place was filled by the C.S.-M. (now Q.M.) Hogarth, of A Company. In fact, after a year abroad, the Battalion lost just a third of its original officers, and about 400 N.C.O.'s and men.

Winter set in early and in its most unpleasant form.

During November there was only one day on which neither rain nor snow fell. The trenches began collapsing at once; after each heavy storm the unrevetted sides fell in, and liquid mud, reaching as high as the thighs, made movement almost impossible; the sump-hole covers floated away, and in the darkness it sometimes happened that a man would be plunged in water up to his neck. Many of the saps were entirely blocked, and at one time it became necessary temporarily to abandon a portion of the front line. Things would have been better if the floor of the trenches had consisted of duckboards (for the bricks so elaborately laid proved mere labour lost), while a proper supply of revetting hurdles could, by the exercise of a little foresight by Corps staff, have been made available. The thigh boots, which gradually arrived in numbers sufficient for men actually in the front line, went far towards preventing wet feet; whale oil was rubbed in, and arrangements made in the village for drying 400 pairs of socks every 24 hours, while the R.A.M.C. provided hot baths in the factory by the pond. Unfortunately, most of the dugouts, after a short resistance, succumbed to the alternations of frost and torrential rain. Sometimes the roof and sides collapsed, as the Oxfords found to their cost when an iron girder killed four men. Sometimes the pressure of water merely caused leakage, but in either case the result was eventually the same. The plight of the men without shelter was often extremely wretched. They lived in water and liquid mud, which mingled with their food and with the fabric of their clothes. However, it was found possible to hold the line more thinly, and during the eight days at Hébuterne no man (except the Machine Gunners) normally spent more than 48 hours in the front line, as only two platoons of each of the two Companies holding the line composed the trench garrison; the remainder stayed in the support dugouts. Platoons were relieved every 24 hours and companies every 48. But the spirit of the men remained unabated, and the rate of sickness surprisingly low; while the mild open weather of January and February brought about a considerable improvement in trench conditions. On the other hand, as the winter drew on the hours of duty in the trenches grew longer and the rests shorter. For instance, during February the Battalion spent 25 days in the trenches and only 4 in reserve. Moreover, the former period was unusually exacting, as we held a more extended front, and the enemy's guns showed violent and continuous activity; while the rest billets, Sailly and Courcelles, were uncomfortable and frequently shelled.

It might have been expected that fighting activity would diminish during this period, but this was far from being the case. Both sides gradually brought up and permanently established in this sector large numbers of big guns; the 9.2-inch and 8-inch howitzers, whose first advent was signalled in the autumn, fired with increasing frequency as stocks of ammunition accumulated. For several consecutive days in February, Hébuterne received a ration of several thousand shells, and cases of shell shock made their appearance. During one of these bombardments Company-Sergt.-Major Lawrence, of B Company, was blown to pieces as he came up from the cellar of the sergeants' mess in the Keep. Although a man of nearly 45 he made light of every hardship; his constant cheerfulness and devotion to duty were an inspiration to all. Intense bombardments of short trench sections also became more common, as the art of raiding, first practised by the Canadians at Messines, developed. The 6th Gloucesters were the first Battalion in our division to indulge in this amusement in November, 1915, when they successfully penetrated the German lines at south-east of Gommecourt Wood. Our Battalion took neither an active nor a passive part in such operations during the winter; their turn was to come, as will be related, on May 16th.

Small encounters between patrols, however, were not infrequent, as the enemy showed increased enterprise, and was no longer willing to surrender tamely command of No-man's Land. On December 14th a patrol of seven men, on reaching the east end of M hedge, were received with bombs and machine-gun fire from the sunken road which ran diagonally between the lines, losing one killed and three wounded. A search party was organised by Captain Blandy, which succeeded in recovering the body of the dead man. Lance-Corpl. Clayton (afterwards 2nd Lieutenant, killed on the Somme), a member of the patrol, though wounded, most gallantly volunteered to lead the search party and covered their withdrawal by throwing bombs. On March 17th, 1916, Lieut. Goolden and Corpl. V. H. Taylor had the satisfaction of shooting two Germans in a mist, who were trying to get back through their own wire; and on returning the patrol picked up an odd assortment of articles, which sound like an extract from some mad auctioneer's catalogue: (1) a glass globe full of liquid with a string net round it; (2) a strong case with powder inside it; (3) six hand grenades; (4) a shoulder strap, silver braid on red cloth, 169 in gilt; (5) a pair of gloves. Scarcely a night passed without fresh ground being covered and new information acquired, which was sometimes of a whimsical character. Once, for instance, an enemy working was heard conversing entirely in English, with such phrases as 'Dig that hole deeper,' 'Bring those stakes along'; one would imagine them to have been a waiters' battalion. Among the most active patrol leaders were Lieuts. Gathorne-Hardy, Lund, Downs, Calder and Teed; the two last-named distinguished themselves by a daylight reconnaissance lasting 3¼ hours in the course of which much information of value was collected.

Nor must we fail to remember with gratitude the three cavalry officers who were attached to us during the winter for periods of one month: Captain A. L. Friend and Lieut. Ansell, of the 7th Dragoon Guards, and Captain M. Simmonds, Indian Cavalry. All did their best to relieve the short-handed company officers, while Captain Simmonds, although a senior captain, took charge of a platoon, and shared all fatigue duties with the subalterns of the Battalion.

When we were back in reserve the various amusements and relaxations, which a stationary warfare permits, were elaborated for the benefit of the men.

Christmas Day was fortunately spent at Authie, and the various companies sat down in comfort in the estaminets to a splendid dinner. Three pigs had been killed for the Battalion's consumption, a plum pudding was presented to each N.C.O. and man by the C.O., and others arrived from the *Daily News* Fund. A tin of cigarettes came from Messrs. H. and G. Simonds', a packet of cigars from the Maidenhead Fund. Each man received a shirt, muffler, socks and chocolate, the produce of a fund most energetically collected from Berkshire by Mrs. Serocold and Mrs. Hedges. The officers spent an equally happy evening at the château, whose owner, Madame De Wailly, kindly provided a room and all other requisites.

A Divisional Football Cup was given by the G.O.C., which was competed for by all units of the 48th Division under Association rules. We were beaten in the first round by the 5th Gloucesters, who scored the winning goal just on time, after an exciting game, in which Sergt. Hedges distinguished himself. The 'Varlets' of the 1st/1st South Midland Field Ambulance, and the Divisional Variety Troupe, of which Private Cooter (B Company) was a well-known member, performed for our benefit, and perhaps most attractive of all was Major Barron's cinematograph entertainment, which was always sure of the warmest reception.

Thus the first winter passed in the normal alternations of trench welfare.

CHAPTER 8

The New Trench and the Raid

The spring of 1916 was slow in coming. The German attack at Verdun had coincided with a long spell of deep snow and bitter cold. An officer going on leave at the end of February vividly remembers his experiences on the frozen roads, and the sight of a column of French troops of all arms 20 miles long, making their way painfully along the great 'Route Nationale' to Amiens to join in the defence of Verdun. But towards the end of March the weather grew warm and genial and the wild daffodils began to appear in all the fields around Sailly. Meanwhile the preliminaries for the Somme offensive became increasingly significant. The forward villages such as Sailly and Bayencourt were cleared of the civil population, and handed over entirely to the Army. Still more monstrous guns came crawling up, and in place of the old battery of 60-pounders, the orchard at the western outskirts of Sailly, in the angle of the Bayencourt road, harboured two 15-inch howitzers. Gun-pits and enormous new dugouts were constructed in Hébuterne. The single-line railway which served the 48th and 4th Division with railheads at Acheux and Louvaincourt was supplemented by numbers of light lines. Troops grew thick upon the ground; the 56th Division appeared upon our left, the 31st on the right, and in May the front held by the Division scarcely exceeded that allotted to a single battalion during the winter. A 4th Army had been formed, of which the 48th Division was on the left in the 10th Corps. Conferences were held by the G.O.C. with C.O.'s and Adjutants two or three times a week, while parties were constantly detailed to witness demonstrations of gas, smoke and flame throwers. At last, also, the drafts so badly needed and so long overdue appeared in fairly adequate numbers; in March alone 202 men joined the Battalion for duty, which brought our total strength up to 874.

Meanwhile the G.O.C. was planning for the execution of the 145th Brigade a task, which sounds prosaic enough on paper, but which demanded for its success minute organisation and a high state of discipline in all concerned—namely, the digging of a forward trench in front of our own wire. Our line between Hébuterne and Serre sagged back in a westerly direction from Trench Hoche to Trench Bouillon, thereby interposing 800-900 yards between ourselves and the Germans, with an intervening rise in No Man's Land. This configuration of the ground presented three obvious defects for offensive operations. It was impossible for the gunners to get direct observation on the sector of enemy trench opposite; it meant that troops deploying for the attack would get out of trenches facing in three directions, and would have to cross an unnecessary depth of shell-swept ground before getting to the assault. It was, therefore, determined to straighten out the line between the two points mentioned above. The battalions concerned assiduously practised wire-cutting, filing silently through the gaps, and night-digging. Our Battalion, which was to find the covering parties, took over the part of the line affected (J Sector, from Serre road to Trench Lassalle) a week beforehand, and every effort was made by means of patrols, two or three of which went out each night, to lo-

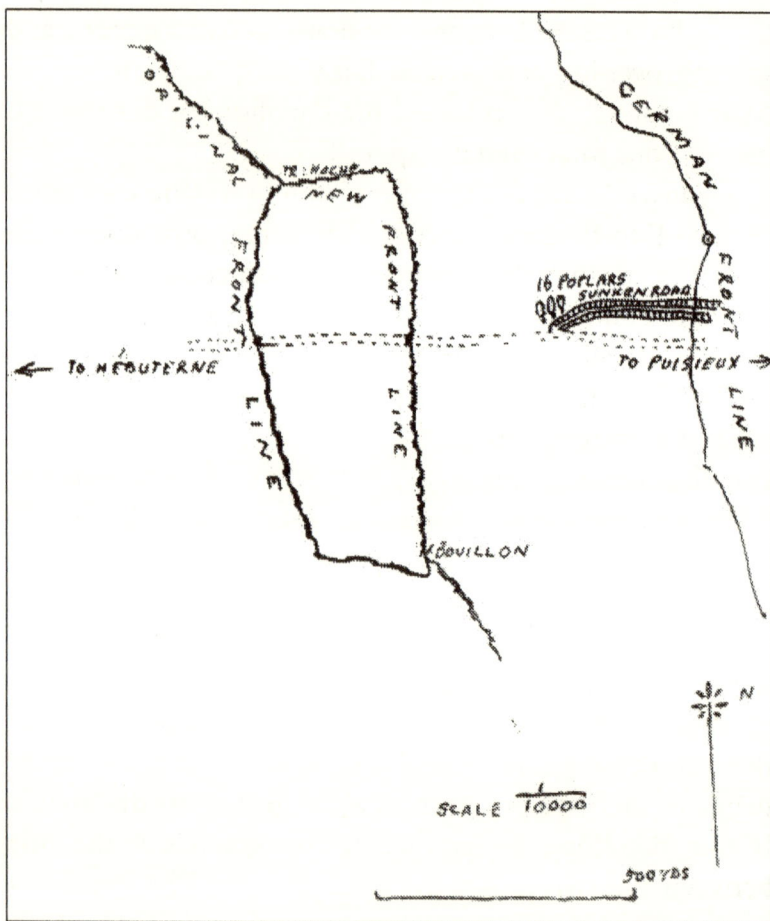

cate any forward posts or rifle pits from which the enemy might get wind of or interfere with the digging of the new trench. On the night of the 9th-10th April the scheme was carried out under the direction of Major Clissold (1st/1st Field Company, South Midland R.E.'s), an unfailing friend of the infantry, who was killed in the autumn of 1917. About 1,500 men in all were engaged; the digging was done by the 4th Oxfords and the 5th Gloucesters, while covering parties and fatigues were provided by the Bucks Battalion and ourselves. About six hours were allotted for the completion of the work, from 9 p.m. to 3 a.m. The moon, which was near the full, shone brilliantly, though at times obscured by clouds, so that there was no fear of the confusion which arises from darkness, but rather of detection by the enemy's posts. Soon after 8.30 p.m. A Company, who were responsible for the protection from the right to the Puisieux road, strung themselves out into groups of three, some 20 yards apart, about 70 paces in front of the tape which marked the course of the proposed trench. While Captain Crouch, of the Bucks, was similarly employed on the left, some of his men, losing touch, ran into the vision of Hun sentries at the Poplars and were received with shots and bombs, which caused uneasy anticipations of discovery, happily unfulfilled. The diggers got to work behind their screen, and ate into the ground with remarkable speed, for stray rounds of shrapnel, intermittent sniping, and the constant discharge of Verey lights throughout the night, suggested that the Hun had some uneasy suspicion that all was not quite as usual; and indeed it seems almost incredible that the clash of the tools, the whispered orders, and the movements of the wiring parties should have entirely failed to strike the ear of a vigilant sentry at 250 yards. By 2 a.m. the work was almost finished; nothing remained but to strengthen the parapet of the new trench and to fill up the spaces between the knife-rests, which defended it some 40 yards in front, with screw pickets and loose strands of wire. By 3.20 a.m. all the diggers had returned to the old line, and the weary covering party, who had lain out for seven tedious hours, came home to get a hot drink, which they had well earned. Only 15 casualties were reported from the whole Brigade, none of which fell to the share of our Battalion. The trench was held by a few posts until dawn and then evacuated. About noon next day an enemy aeroplane flew along it, and the observer could be plainly seen leaning out and taking photographs of this mushroom growth. Almost immediately every battery from La Brayelle to Serre began to register upon it, and for weeks it was rendered unwholesome by the constant attention of artillery and mine-throwers. A poem of Lieut. Downs' preserves the air of mystery in which the whole scheme was so fortunately conceived and executed.

A whisper wandered round
Of a plan of the G. O. C.'s,
And figures surveyed the ground
In stealthy groups of threes;
But the whole Brigade were there,
Or pretty well all the lot,
When we dug the trench at Never-mind-where,
On April the Never mind-what.

The What's-a-names dug the trench,
The Who-is-its found the screen,
And we mustn't forget to mench
The Thingumies in between;
The Tothermies built the fence,
And the R.E.'s "also ran,"
For we didn't spare any expense,
With labour a shilling a man.

There isn't much else to tell,
Though the enemy made a song,
And tried to blow it to Hell,
But got the address all wrong;
For you'll find it's still out there
In the bally old self-same spot,
That trench which we built at Never-mind-where,
On April the Never-mind-what.

After these excitements the Battalion moved back on the 12th, half to Sailly, half to the huts in the park of Couin Château, which were leaky and surrounded by a pathless morass of mud several inches deep. Here the Battalion was reinoculated, as 18 months had elapsed since the original dose was injected in the autumn of 1914, and spent its mornings in Platoon and Company Drill, until its return to J Sector on the 20th. There was plenty of work and little comfort in the line that tour. The conditions resembled those of the winter at their worst; in the new trench, hastily dug and unrevetted, water and mud engulfed the passer-by to the waist. One afternoon a German was reported to have got in, and the Adjutant (Lieut. Ridley) who happened to be on the spot, at once organised a bombing party to deal with him, but after wading laboriously to the point indicated, found that the bird had flown. Meanwhile, the Huns showed their displeasure by sending into the sector 500-1,000 shells every day, and casualties were naturally higher than the normal, including Lieut. Duff seriously wounded, and Lieut. Calder shell-shock. No one was therefore sorry when on the 25th we returned to Authie, after an interval of three months, to the great delight of the inhabitants, and enjoyed the spring for a short while in that pleasant valley. Before returning to the line the battalion spent a few days at Sailly and Couin, furnishing working parties for Hébuterne each night and day. On May 8th we relieved the

4th Oxfords in G Sector on the extreme right of the Brigade front. This tour was destined to be memorable in the history of the Battalion. The ground was entirely new to us, and extremely difficult. All rations and supplies had to be brought up from Hébuterne by communication trenches more than a mile long and in bad repair. The whole sector had been the scene of a fierce battle in June 1915, for the possession of Touvent Farm and the outskirts of Serre, and was everywhere cut up by old disused trenches, French and German, and shell holes, and was still littered with bones and skulls. Nor was the front line more attractive; it formed a sharp salient projecting towards Serre, held by disconnected posts, ill defended, close to the enemy, and joined to the support line by only two communication trenches, one at each side of the salient. So vague and difficult of identification was this line of posts that Captain Cruttwell, when visiting them for the first time, nearly walked into the German lines while trying to establish connection with D Company, until warned of his mistake by a shower of rifle-grenades. The whole sector, indeed, closely resembled the crater areas, which the experiences of the Somme were to render familiar. The first week in this dreary spot passed uneventfully; the enemy guns and *minenwerfer*, the latter of the largest calibre, whose explosion was deafening, were active, but not unusually so, and up to the 15th the Battalion could congratulate themselves on an absence of casualties during the tour. They were to be relieved next day, and it seemed that the trouble always expected here would be reserved for others. During the 15th, however, the usual shelling seemed to the two Company Commanders in the front line—Captain Cruttwell, of B, and Captain Attride, of D, to be more methodical and to suggest a registration on all tactical points. Still this impression was not definite enough to arouse serious foreboding. Up to midnight all was quiet. Then a heavy bombardment opened upon the 56th Division on the left; our divisional guns, who were helping to cover that sector, opened at once in response to the S.O.S. The two anxious Company Commanders felt convinced that if a raid was intended they would not be the victims of it. But as soon as our guns were securely switched off on to a false target, the enemy showed his hand. His guns ceased to play on the 56th Division and were directed with extreme violence against our front. It was then 12.30 a.m. on the morning of May 16th; the raid had begun. It is now necessary, in order to understand its course, to describe minutely, with the aid of the map, the dispositions of the two Companies affected. The length of the line was approximately 1,200 yards; on the right B Company had two platoons in the front line strung out into seven posts between Nairne and Wrangel, each containing from six to nine men. Two sections and a Lewis gun team were in Jones Street, which had been chosen as the main defensive line in case of attack. The remaining two sections with another Lewis gun were in Caber, and the fourth platoon in Worcester Street. Company Headquarters were established some 800 yards behind the front line, at Pimlico, where a platoon of A Company was placed in dugouts at the disposal of O.C. Company. The line of D Company on the left stretched from Wrangel to Jena, and was similarly held by two platoons furnishing eight posts. The supporting platoon on the right was equally divided between Trench Dominique and Oxford Street; that on the left was located in the forward end of Jena. Company Headquarters were in Vauban, and Captain Attride disposed of a reserve platoon of C Company in Vercingetorix. Further two platoons of C Company which were returning from a working party in Wrangel when the bombardment started, were placed in dugouts near Pimlico.

16TH MAY, 1916

The plan of the bombardment, which was a master-piece of method, was as follows:—From 12.30 to 1 a.m. the whole of our front and supervision line was bombarded with field guns, 5.9-inch howitzers and mine-throwers; but the chief intensity of fire was directed at B Company between Nairne and Chasseur Hedge, with the object, which was practically accomplished, of destroying or burying all the posts included therein. At 1 a.m. a red rocket was shot up from the enemy lines, and the fire from Nairne to Wrangel lifted, but fell with redoubled fury on the support and reserve lines, where every communication trench and dugout was deluged with shells. At Pimlico, in particular, 5.9-inch shells were thrown at the rate of 100 a minute, enveloping it in a dense fog of smoke and fumes, and the supporting platoon of A Company lost nearly half its strength. Meanwhile the fire on either flank covered both front line and support, rendering lateral communication impossible. Thus B Company was isolated, and the enemy infantry immediately entered. Post No. 7 opposed their entry, but was overpowered—none of the nine men who composed it were ever seen again, but the ground about was afterwards found littered with exploded and unexploded German bombs, showing that they had fought a good fight. The Germans then divided into two parties with separate tasks. One party worked along Jones Street towards the right, some moving in the trench, some along the parados. They destroyed the left post in Jones Street, but were eventually checked by Lance-Corpl. Cooke with his Lewis Gun team, which, reflecting the coolness of its commander, kept up a steady rifle fire when the gun jammed. The Huns then retired and left Jones Street at the point of entry, after fulfilling what was presumably their job of protecting their comrades from attack in the rear. For the other party, working along the fire trench, attacked Posts 6-2 inclusive from the rear. These posts were in sore straits. Their defences had been blown to pieces, their rifles damaged, broken or buried, and their bombs scattered; they had themselves been shaken or buried and were left defenceless. The story of a survivor from Post 2, who escaped, will serve as an example. As they endeavoured to extricate themselves and their weapons from the wrecked post, Germans appeared behind them and ordered them in English to mount the parapet or they would be shot. Private Chapman at once tackled an officer with his fists and, shot by the latter's revolver, died most bravely. Four men were taken, and one alone escaped. However, 12 survivors in all reached Post 1, which remained intact and resisted stoutly. Here Lieut. Ward, who was on duty, took charge, and reorganised the 12, only to find that some were wounded, and that the rifles of the remainder were useless. Accordingly he withdrew towards Nairne, and was fortunate to get them back safely, for at one point four Germans peered into the trench, which was a very deep one, close to the party, but made off when Ward loosed his revolver at them. Meanwhile, No. 1 Post, under Sergt. Holloway, a brave soldier from Abingdon, facing both to front and rear, drove back all the enemy who approached them with rifle and bombs, and effectively staved off their progress towards Nairne, where the position was secured by a post of 13th West Yorks (31st Division) which was promptly moved to the left in answer to Lieut. Ward's request. The support platoon was organised for defence in Caber by Lieut. Field, who remained with his men though seriously wounded. Here he was found by Lieut. Gathorne-Hardy, who, with his usual contempt for danger, had volunteered to go up from Company Headquarters to re-establish connection, which had been broken within five minutes of the commencement of the bombardment.

While B Company was being attacked, fire was still di-

Lieut.-Col. R. J. Clarke, C.M.G., D.S.O., T.D.
Commanding from 14 Feb. 1916 To 13th April, 1918

rected with violence on the front line of the left Company, and continued until 1.40 a.m., when it also lifted on to the support and reserve areas. The damage here had been mainly confined to Posts 1-3, where all the men had been killed or buried; at Post 1 five men were saved by the systematic and collected courage of Private Appleby (4749), who dug them out one after the other. At Post 3, Captain Boyle and Sergt. Pitman dug out Lance-Corpl. Sargeant and the other men, being disturbed during the operation by the appearance of a German on the parapet, whom they shot and wounded. Lance-Corpl. Sargeant was no sooner extricated than he collected bombs, and returned to his post only to find two wounded comrades being hauled off by a party of Germans. They received his bombs into their midst and ran back into the darkness behind Chasseur Hedge, where their supports were waiting. Meanwhile, Posts 4 and 5 remained intact and full of fight. Singing in the intervals between firing:

Pack up your troubles in your old kit-bag,
And smile, smile, smile. . . .

they held off the enemy, who could be dimly seen filing through their wire and forming up outside in three lines, distinguished by white armlets. Post 5 soon received a reinforcement of some 20 men under Sergt. V. H. Taylor, who came up from Oxford Street. They had been summoned by Corpl. Page, a most gallant Wokingham man, who volunteered to go back through the fiery curtain of the barrage, which task he accomplished without harm. No further attack was made upon D Company, which escaped with comparatively light casualties. Captain Boyle was afterwards awarded the M.C. for the skill and coolness with which he organised the defence of his sector, and Corpl. Sargeant the Military Medal. The bombardment continued unabated until 2.45, and then ceased suddenly with the first light of dawn. The ruinous state of the trenches made daylight movement difficult and dangerous, as the enemy fired rifle grenades continually at broken points in the communication trenches, causing several casualties among men who were not quick enough in running the gauntlet. In spite of such difficulties all the wounded were evacuated by 10 a.m., though in some cases it took four hours to get the stretcher from the front line to the dressing station in the village. The losses had been heavy, amounting in all to 98, of whom 18 were killed and 29 missing; of these B Company supplied 60, thus losing half of its fighting strength. Many hours were spent next night by parties left behind after the relief of the Battalion in search of the missing, who afterwards were almost without exception reported as prisoners of war. This eventful night was the last spent by the Battalion in the trenches for five weeks; the 48th Division, which had established a record for an unbroken length of service in the line, was being withdrawn into Army Reserve. Thus the Battalion came through their first serious test, and were not found wanting. The praise which Colonel Clarke bestowed next day at Couin on their endurance, discipline and fighting spirit, was repeated by the Divisional General and the Corps Commander.

CHAPTER 9

Before the Battle

The day at Couin was spent in packing and loading up, a task rendered easier by the loan from our good friends, 3rd Warwick Battery, of two G.S. wagons. Early on the 18th we joined the Brigade at St. Leger and marched to Beauval. The day was very hot. The march was mainly through narrow valleys, dense with dust. The Battalion were short of sleep, and very weary, while the sun beat down upon their steel helmets, which they wore for the first time on the march. None the less, Sir A. Hunter-Weston complimented Colonel Clarke on the way in which they marched past him at Marieux. Beauval was reached at noon, a quiet little country town, with long shady streets; and the billets were very good. The fortnight here was spent in route marches, grouping practices at the range, and platoon and company training in general. The keen pleasure with which the men turned to drill and small company schemes after the months of trench monotony was very noticeable. A splendid compliment was paid to D Company by the Corps Commander, who met them one day on the march. Stopping their commander, Captain Attride, he said that he had never seen a finer body of men in France; that he was proud of them, and that they had every right to be proud of themselves, for their conduct on the night of the 16th.

On the 31st the Brigade made an early start, rising at dawn and moving off at 4 a.m. in a bright, fresh, lovely morning, well-suited for the long march to the St. Riquier training area. The Battalion arrived at their billets, the small village of Maison Roland, some 7 miles north-east of Abbeville, before midday. The inhabitants, who had been unfortunate in the troops quartered on them just before, showed some hostility, closing their houses, and refusing to allow the men to enter. All ill-feeling, however, was rapidly removed. Colonel Clarke had warned the Battalion to do everything to create a good impression, and when we left the Mayor sent a letter thanking all ranks for their behaviour. The whole neighbourhood was a mass of troops rehearsing the Somme battles on specially prepared areas, where officers remarked on the advantage of being able to move freely without fear of damaging the crops. Some days in succession were spent in Battalion, Brigade and Divisional Training, and all learnt by experience how much the inevitable stagnation and immobility of long-continued trench warfare dull the initiative and lessen the quickness of mind and body. The days were strenuous; réveillé, as a rule, was at 4 a.m., and work began at 6 and lasted until 1, leaving the afternoons free, while the nights were twice begun with Brigade attacks, and finished in bivouac. But the men enjoyed their time; they grew hard for battle, with supple limbs and the indescribable thrill of perfect physical fitness. And in spite of the hard work time was found for recreation; cricket was played again for the first time since the summer days at Hébuterne in 1915, and a Brigade Horse Show created keen interest. In St. Riquier men from all the Division could foregather in the estaminets, one of which possessed a much-coveted billiard table, and sometimes it was even possible to spend a day in the pleasant town of Abbeville.

For the latter part of this training period the Battalion had moved to Gapennes, a village some 6 miles north of Maison Roland, where, as before, hostility shown at arrival was soon changed to friendliness and goodwill.

On June 10th the Battalion set its face again towards the east; and after two days' long and dusty marching we found ourselves again in the huts of Couin, which next day were exchanged for an undesirable and filthy bivouac at Sailly. The preparations of the last month had completely changed the aspect of these forward villages, and it was clear that the time was at hand. Sailly was full of camps and dumps; the bare and desolate slopes to the east harboured tier upon tier of guns. Reliefs from the Brigade worked day and night without a pause in Hébuterne and the adjacent trenches. When the Battalion took over H. Sector on the 16th, they found every nook and corner of the trenches by night filled with parties digging new dugouts and Stokes mortar emplacements, bringing up gas-cylinders, smoke candles and all the diverse paraphernalia of the modern offensive; while the enemy's artillery and machine guns incessantly harassed these suspected activities. Otherwise, no incident of especial note occurred during this tour, except a forced landing by one of our machines in front of Puisieux, which drew immediately into the open a mob of inquisitive Germans estimated at several hundreds. The 24th found the battalion back at Couin, where they were to stay until the fateful 1st July. The damp, ill-ventilated and crowded huts were responsible for a good many cases of sore throat and rheumatism. But there was little time to be sick. In the interval between working parties, bayonet fighting and wire-cutting, the last and most significant preparations for attack were made. Blue hearts, the distinguishing mark of the Battalion, were sewn on to the back of the steel helmet cover, and tin triangles affixed to the haversack, which was to be worn on the back in fighting order. It may be of interest to give in detail the equipment with which the men went into battle. Two sandbags were tucked in front of the belt; one Mills bomb was in each of the bottom pockets of the tunic; 50 extra rounds of ammunition were slung in a bandolier over the right shoulder. In his haversack each man carried one iron ration, cardigan waistcoat, soft cap, and pair of socks; the waterproof sheet was folded and strapped on outside, and the mess-tin fastened to the lowest buckle of the haversack. Every other man carried a pick or shovel slung; and the Brigade, with a more intimate solicitude, advised all ranks to carry a pipe, matches and tobacco.

The bombardment had begun on the 25th, and night after night from the hilltop at Couin watchers saw with exultation and confident expectation, reflected in many letters, the great shells picking out the enemy's lines with fire.

On July 1st the 48th Division were in Corps Reserve, and took no part in the battle, with the exception of the 5th and 6th Warwicks, who covered themselves with glory in Serre, though suffering terrible losses, which included both their commanding officers. The Division was concentrated for the day round Mailly-Maillet, which we reached about 1 p.m. after numberless checks in the encumbered roads. Detachments of Indian Cavalry were resting their horses by the roadside as we passed through Bus. The rest of the day was spent in bivouac in an open field; the guns around fired incessantly, including a 15-inch close at hand, but no hostile shell fell near. We were about 3 miles west of Beaumont-Hamel, where the 29th Division were so furiously engaged. All the good news of the morning, the taking of Gommecourt Cemetery and of Serre, had fired expectation, and the disappointment was correspondingly bitter when it was known at nightfall that the 8th Army Corps were everywhere back in their original front line. Next morning the Brigade received orders to attack early on the 3rd, their objective being south of Beaumont-Hamel and beyond the Ancre brook, a piece of country which none of them had seen before. The Brigadier, with the Commanding Officers, tried to get forward during the day and pick up the lie of the land, but the shelling, smoke and dust made observation impossible. The Brigade, therefore, moved up that night to Mesnil, a small ruined village 1 mile behind the line, very much in the dark. As they moved in, many smelt for the first time the curious fragrant odour of lachrymatory gas, which seemed to come from the flowers of some wayside garden until the pricking and watering at the eyes proved otherwise. The Company Commanders went forward into the trenches to find out what they could; to their right loomed a great black mass, and they debated whether it was a hill or a cloud. Suddenly an array of lights and a flicker of rifle-fire running along the top revealed it as the steep western slopes of Thiepval. A Company was just filing into the trenches when a rumour was brought by Lieut. Hughes that the attack was cancelled; inquiries were made and its truth confirmed. The Battalion returned the way it had come and bivouacked again in Mailly-Maillet at daybreak. The men, who had moved out in high spirits, were greatly cast down by this conclusion. It is, however, a matter for congratulation that the Battalion was not called upon to make its first attack under circumstances so unfavourable on positions which had defied the elaborate preparations which preceded the assault on July 1st. Next day guns and limbers passed in a steady stream going south—a sure indication that all efforts were being concentrated in widening the breach already made. That evening the Battalion returned to the huts at Couin much depressed at the prospect of taking up again the drab monotony of trench life after hopes aroused in the last few days. The weather now became very bad with almost incessant rain, and we relieved the 5th Gloucesters on July 8th in trenches waist deep in water, badly damaged by the bombardment, and affording the depressing view to right and left of the dead of the 31st and 56th Divisions lying out unburied. Meanwhile a great show of activity was kept up to foster among the enemy the idea that further attacks were intended; new stores of smoke bombs were sent up with instructions when and how to let them off, which were invariably cancelled before performance. Another assaulting trench was dug by the Brigade, running some 700 yards south of that already described, for which the Battalion supplied a small covering party of 50 men, who suffered a few casualties in the bright moonlight. The weather fortunately improved, and we were able to hand over the trenches to the 5th Gloucesters on July 12th dry and in good repair. Next day 100 men went over to see the 5th Battalion in the Bois de Warnimont. Thirteen months ago they had come to us for their first experience of trench warfare; this time a small remnant, they were resting from their attack on Ovillers, where every officer except the C.O. had been killed or wounded. We were now immediately to follow them into battle, for next day a fleet of motor-'buses bore us south to the crowded village of Senlis behind the Ovillers—La Boisselle Sector of the Somme front.

CHAPTER 10

The July Fighting at Pozières

The successful night attack of July 14th had eaten into the third German line between Longueval and Bazentin-le-Petit on a front of some three miles. The principal British efforts for the next six weeks were consequently directed towards getting more elbow-room on both flanks. On the north progress had been greatly hindered by the stubborn resistance of the German Guards at Ovillers, which was not cleared up till July 11th. Our line now skirted the southern orchards of Pozières, running westwards just north of Ovillers and then curving sharply back to the old front line near Authuille. All this sector was, to our great disadvantage, overlooked and enfiladed by the height of Thiepval; and progress, though steady, was for the most part slow and heavily bought.

On this occasion the Battalion was given ample time to view and get familiar with the ground, as the attack did not take place until July 23rd. Soon after arrival at Senlis the officers went over to La Boisselle. This first sight of the devastated area created the deepest impression. Afterwards such complete destruction became common enough; but till then no one had seen a village literally blown away. Not only the walls, but the very brick dust had vanished; its site could be fixed only by reference to the map and to the

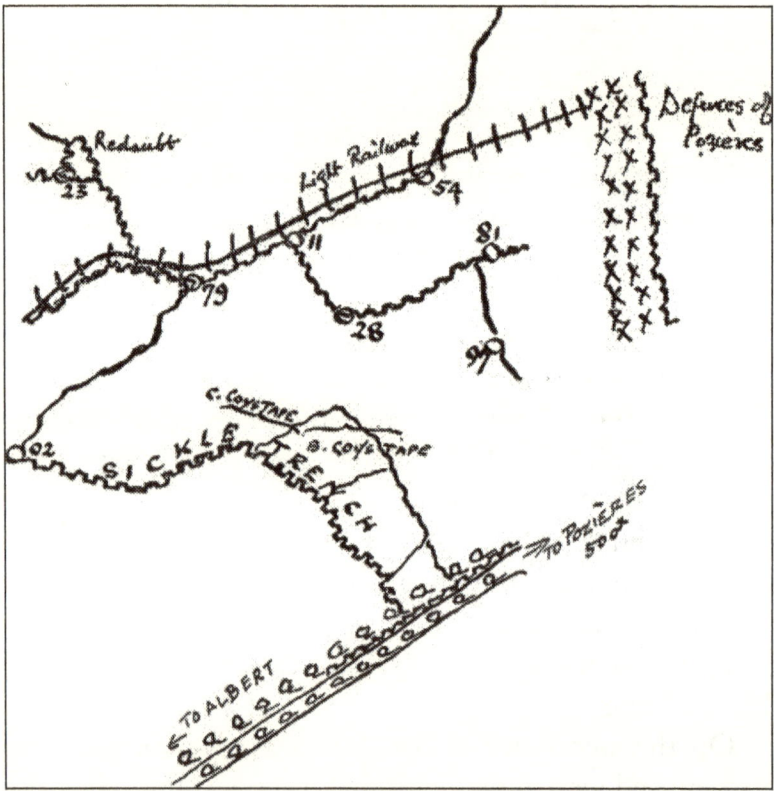

board stating "This is La Boisselle." Every kind of battle-wreckage lay about, including many dead bodies, ten days unburied in the midsummer heat. But though the guns had done their work so well, enough remained of the wonderful fortified labyrinth to suggest the difficulties of attacking troops. The Battalion moved up by degrees, bivouacking on the 18th east of Albert in support of the Oxfords; and taking over trenches west of Pozières next night from 7th Royal Warwicks. Only two platoons of B Company held the short front line; which was naturally of a rough and ready description, shallow and blocked in places by earth or bodies. The enemy, in hourly anticipation of attack, were very restless; their infantry, who appeared to be very thick on the ground, sent up showers of lights and fired at intervals throughout the night hours. Their guns, mostly 5.9-inch and 8-inch, fired almost incessantly; even a comparative lull, it was remarked, would have been counted a heavy bombardment in the old quiet days. Many gas shells were used, mainly on road junctions and assembly points in the rear. We had only some seven casualties from this source—our support and reserve companies moved up or down constantly in accordance with the ever-shifting situations. Battalion Headquarters remained in a German dugout in La Boisselle. Though tainted by the foul reek from the village, it earned the admiration of its tenants by its solid and elaborate construction.

The 21st was a day of great activity, stores were brought up all day, and the trenches improved for the attack as far as intense enemy fire would permit. Lieut. Downs that night took out a patrol from the right, who explored the south-west corner of Pozières in spite of the extreme alertness of the Huns, and returned safely with the most valuable information for which the Anzacs, over whose attacking frontage the patrol had gone, were most grateful. Everyone was glad to have them on our flank, for they were splendid men, full of confidence and keenness.

Next day detailed orders were issued for the attack of the 145th Brigade. The two assaulting Battalions, 4th Oxfords and 5th Gloucesters, were allotted a frontage of about 500 yards a-piece. The right flank of the Oxfords rested on the Anzacs at a point some 500 yards west of Pozières. We were in support to the Oxfords, and, therefore, concerned only with their objectives. To understand the events of the following day it is necessary closely to study the map. The irregular curve of Sickle Trench, prolonged along the north side of the main road, constituted our front line. The Huns held a somewhat similar line, with a marked southward bulge; the Oxfords had orders to take the whole of this trench from Point 81 to Point 11. The difficulties of a simultaneous attack on such a pronounced salient are obvious, and were increased by the trench running southward from Point 81 for 150 yards, which terminated in a hostile strong point at 97.

The Oxfords attacked at dawn, but were immediately pressed at both flanks, and began to be squeezed into the centre near Point 28. B Company (Captain Aldworth) and C. Company (Captain Lewis), Royal Berks, had come up the main road under cover of darkness and were deployed by 3.30 a.m. (summer time), along a tape running east and west some 250 yards south of the centre of the Oxfords' objective. Here they waited for information and orders. It was still twilight and no certain information could be gained. Shots were now heard intermittently, and wounded men came back, telling, as wounded men will, contradictory stories. Some said that the Oxfords were wiped out; others that they had captured the trench. Two men were sent forward to reconnoitre, and came back to report that the position was critical. It was now 3.55 a.m.; the day was coming and the enemy barrage was growing more intense. Captain Aldworth at once ordered the two Companies to go forward to the assistance of the Oxfords. For this prompt decision, which undoubtedly secured the success of the whole operation, and for his bravery throughout, Captain Aldworth was awarded the M.C. The two Companies now advanced into the captured trench, losing some men en route from shell fire, especially on the right, where 2nd Lieut. Clayton was killed. During the advance B Company got split in two, Nos. 5 and 8 Platoons being divided by C Company from Nos. 6 and 7, who entered the left of the trench with Captain Aldworth. The congestion of the men of the two Battalions in the centre of the shallow trench was great, and there could be no security until the flanks were cleared and made good. Point 97 was soon gained, and Lieut. Downs pushed resolutely forward beyond 81, endeavouring to get in touch with the Australians. He reached the heavily-wired German second line, which ran north and south through the outskirts of Pozières, but was forced back. Returning with about 20 men from all three Companies he barricaded and secured Point 81, after killing 11 Germans in hand-to-hand fighting and capturing 2. Meanwhile, Point 11 was attacked on two sides. When the left of B Company got into the trench some Germans were still in view running away towards the left, one of whom Captain Aldworth bayoneted himself. Lieut. Tripp at once followed them up and bombed them out of Point 11 with the assistance of a party under Lieut. Wakeford, who jumped out of the centre and led them fearlessly over the open to the disputed place. Lieut. Wakeford was shot dead just as he reached his objective, but his action was entirely successful. By 6 a.m. the situation was reported safe, and the men still crowded and mixed up, were able to start consolidating and deepening the trench. At 6.30 a.m. about 200 men appeared over the brow of the hill on the left, where it dips down towards Ovillers, advancing with fixed bayonets. It was a Company of the Bucks moving in perfect order and with great fire. As they reached the trenches east of Point 11 the Huns could be seen coming out of their dugouts and flying in all directions, many with their hands up. A Lewis gun from C Company opened on those who tried to bolt back northwards, but soon stopped, as it was clear that they could not escape the Bucks. Captain Lewis went up to meet the Bucks officer, and they decided on Point 11 as a division between the two Battalions. The morning passed quietly, with no more than intermittent sniping on both sides, in which Sergt. Giles accounted for several Huns. Thanks to the excellent organisation of Captain Attride, parties from D Company brought up all that was required in the way of bombs, sandbags and so forth. By 10 o'clock the trenches had been reduced to a decent order, and the men were able to eat their breakfasts. At noon the Oxfords, who had been moving away to the right, took over from 81-97; B Company carried on the line to a large bush near 28, which had escaped the bombardment, and from there C Company extended to the Bucks' right flank. This sorting out had scarcely been accomplished when the enemy started a heavy bombardment, which lasted until 5 p.m. For the last two hours in particular it was of extreme violence, and fell chiefly on B Company. Here in the ruinous and improvised trenches very great damage was done, and more than 50 per cent of the Company were put out of action. Many of the carrying parties from D Company had also been hit, and lay in the open. Private C. J. Sadler, from Wokingham, a Company Stretcher-Bearer, dressed them all, and put them into shell holes until nightfall. In the performance of these very brave actions three of his ribs were broken by a shell. He was subsequently awarded the D.C.M.

Meanwhile touch had been established with the Anzacs. News of their progress had been sought throughout the day with great eagerness. They had been seen in the morning by D Company making their way through the ruins of Pozières; and later on the fires which they imperturbably lit on the captured ground to fry their bacon, had drawn heavy shell-fire on the whole area. But it was not until the afternoon that a more or less continuous line was linked up. The violence of the shelling suggested a counter-attack after dark, which it would be difficult to repel with the greatly reduced forces available. There was great joy, therefore, when Captain Aldworth returned from a journey to Battalion Headquarters at 6.30 p.m. with the news that the Battalion would be relieved that night by the 5th Warwicks. The two Companies stood-to from dark onwards, but no attack developed. There was an anxious moment for C Company when a bomb exploded close to 2nd Lieut. Beazley in the trench. He had just come up to join his Company and was hard at work digging. A light was sent up and showed the ground in front to be clear; the bomb had evidently been buried in the trench and went off when struck by a shovel. Lieut. Beazley was fortunate to escape with some severe bruises. The relief was begun at 10.30 p.m., and the weary men were able to get a short rest by sleeping in the old German line south of Ovillers. The rest was, however, a very short one, for by 1.30 p.m. next day the Battalion were back in the trenches, which they had taken over from the Bucks, immediately to the left of their former line. They were alloted a frontage of about 400 yards, spanning the head of the shallow valley running down to Ovillers; between the lines ran the almost obliterated tracks of a light railway.

About 200 yards north of the left of our line a German strong point on higher ground looked into and enfiladed the whole of the captured ground, and D Company was ordered to attack it at 1.50 a.m. next morning. Colonel Clarke was able to make his arrangements direct with the artillery through Major Todd, the forward liaison officer, much to their mutual satisfaction. The batteries concerned gave a five-minutes intensive bombardment with wonderful accuracy in the darkness. This, however, was the only part of the attack which was destined to go smoothly, for the enemy replied at once by a furious artillery and machine-gun fire, causing many casualties, and made it almost impossible for the attack to develop. One bombing party pushed forward a few yards, only to lose every man but two from a concentrated shower of rifle grenades. The Germans, in fact, were in great force, and held every approach to the strong point resolutely. All chance of surprise had gone, and the C.O. therefore refused Captain Attride's request to be allowed to make a new attack. Indeed, at daybreak the German bombardment, which had died down, restarted with a violence which kept on increasing until 5.15 a.m., when a bombing attack was made on 13 and 14 Platoons at the road barricade. 2nd Lieuts. Taylor and Cooke (the latter having come up with supports) kept up a hot fire with rifle grenades and by their action and example drove back the enemy. C.S.M. Rider, who had joined the Battalion not long before, had the first opportunity of showing that combination of bravery and capacity which afterwards earned him a M.C. After the counter-attack had been repulsed there remained only a few hours to hold on until the 5th Gloucesters relieved us, and we were able to get back to bivouacs near Albert to enjoy a hot meal and fall asleep.

Such were the fortunes of the Battalion in their first attack. Their losses for the six days spent under continuous heavy fire were, if judged by the standards of this present war, very moderate. Three officers, 2nd Lieuts. Wakeford,

Clayton and Teed, were killed, and three wounded (2nd Lieuts. Down, Taylor and Kenney). The losses among other ranks amounted to 230, of whom only 27, a singularly low proportion, were killed. The total number who went into action was about 650.

I will close this chapter with a short quotation from the special order of the day on these operations by Colonel Clarke, whose words of praise were fully endorsed by the Divisional and the Corps Commanders.

'It will be a matter of great pride for all who know or are connected with the Battalion to hear of the gallant way in which the Company Officers led the attacks, and the able way in which they handled their various commands; of the contempt for danger and ready resource shown by all the N.C.O.'s, and the bravery, extreme steadiness and coolness in which the lines advanced across the open to the attack or held the captured trenches under the heavy machine-gun fire, and during the counter-attack.'

The acts of individual gallantry and devotion were many and conspicuous. Some have already been mentioned in the course of this narrative, and a full list will be found at the end of the book.

CHAPTER 11

Rest and Battle

The Battalion stood greatly in need of a respite from fighting. As we have seen, it had lost rather more than a third of its fighting strength. It is true that numbers had been practically maintained by a succession of drafts, but time was required to assimilate these men into the companies, and to complete their training, which was in some respects seriously deficient. Conscription had only come into operation in the spring, and voluntary supplies had fallen very low; the wastage of the first two months of the Somme had therefore to be made good by men whose average length of service was no more than three months. Some of them were by no means familiar with the handling or mechanism of their rifles, and knew nothing about a bomb, while their marching powers, as tested by the hot July sun and the dusty roads, fell short of the required standard. The Companies, also, which had suffered very unequally in the fighting, required considerable reorganisation, while many fresh N.C.O.'s had to be created, and made familiar with their duties as far as the short time available permitted.

The Brigade made a long two days' journey from Bouzincourt, a crowded little village west of Albert, through Beauval, where the inhabitants welcomed us for one night in our old billets, to Cramont. Here, in glorious midsummer weather the Battalion spent ten days enjoying with an intense pleasure, after the blasted and featureless battle front, the peacefulness of a charming village, with green fields and trees, almost beyond the sound of the guns. The whole of this period was allotted to Company Training, and many hours were spent in bayonet fighting and bombing. Every man, indeed, threw at least two live bombs, a practice which proved of the greatest value in the August fighting ahead.

Major Barron's cinematograph and Divisional Band made their reappearance, to the general pleasure; whilst all clothing received a much-needed disinfecting from a travelling thresher. The brief interlude was soon over. On 9th August the Battalion moved back in the same direction, though a detour caused by blocked roads, lengthened the return journey to three days. Bouzincourt was now the daily target of long-range guns, and as cellar room was very limited it was thought prudent for the Battalion to bivouac outside the village on the Senlis road. The Division was returning to exactly the same sector west of Pozières, where the 12th Division had been operating during our absence. The difficulties of the uphill advance may be estimated by the fact that the line had been advanced barely half a mile during that period. On the night of the 12th, however, our 5th Battalion, taking the Huns by surprise, won an important success by taking Ridge Trench or 6th Avenue, at the crest of the long slope, with a view northward and eastward. This they accomplished at the incredibly low cost of three casualties. Three platoons of the Oxfords crawled up in daylight next morning and successfully relieved them without incident. The remainder of that day passed quietly; the Battalion were in dugouts round the southern and eastern outskirts of Ovillers, in support to the Oxfords, comparatively comfortable and secure, and expecting no immediate call. But they were to undergo within 24 hours by far their severest ordeal since they landed in France.

The first hint of trouble came at 9.30 p.m. that evening, when a message from the Oxfords stated that the enemy were trying to bomb them out of the trench. An hour later the Brigade ordered bombs to be sent up, and Nos. 1 and 2 Platoons, under Lieut. Garside, were sent forward. It was at that time intended that the Oxfords themselves should undertake the counter-attack; but Sergt. Taylor went to the Oxford Headquarters to maintain close touch between the two Battalions. At 12.50 a.m. D Company were similarly put by the Brigade under the orders of Colonel Bartlett, and left with a further supply of bombs. Colonel Clarke realised that the situation was becoming more serious, and that further help might be demanded of him, though he was at present assured that one Company would be sufficient. The other two Companies were accordingly warned to be in instant readiness, and Captain Lewis moved C Company out of their dugouts into one of the communication trenches leading up to the Oxfords' Headquarters, which were in the line captured by the Bucks on July 23rd. Here they waited after bombs and a bandolier a-piece had been served out. Two hours passed in uncertainty. But at 2.50 a.m. an unwelcome message was received from Colonel Bartlett, asking Colonel Clarke if he would undertake the counter-attack. The latter most naturally refused, on the ground that Colonel Bartlett was on the spot, knew the ground (which our Battalion had never seen), and had his own Battalion with 1-1/2 of our Companies. The Brigadier, however, finding that the Oxfords were not in a position to take the action required, owing to their losses, made a virtue of necessity, and ordered Colonel Clarke to do so as soon as possible.

It was now 3 a.m.; the Oxford Headquarters had already told us that 1-1/2 hours would be quite sufficient to get the Battalion into its assaulting position. The attack was therefore fixed for 4.45 a.m., and a 7-minutes barrage arranged with the artillery. C Company and the remaining two platoons of A began their journey forward with all speed, though time was found to give each man his tot of rum before starting. They reached Point 18 on the place of assembly (which will be remembered as the junction between Bucks and Berks on July 23rd) about 4.15. Here Colonel Clarke found the Company Commanders with Captain Pickford, of the Oxfords. The latter gave them the disastrous information that another hour would be required to get into position instead of the half hour previously estimated. Colonel Clarke instantly went back to Oxford Headquarters to make the necessary alterations with the artillery, and to secure a barrage commencing at 5.15 a.m. Meanwhile the Companies doubled up, with C leading and A in the rear. The need for haste was most urgent, for the day was breaking and the trench was seriously battered. The men crouched low as they ran, but the Hun probably saw their heads, for shrapnel was sprinkled along the communication trench, causing a few casualties. As Captain Blandy (O.C. A Company) approached the head of the communication trench in broad daylight, he looked at his watch and found it was already 5.10 a.m. His remaining two platoons were waiting for him, lying low in the trench, very weary, for they had been carrying all night. They got up and followed along at the rear of the Company. Turning right-handed they entered a vacant and much-broken fire trench. A man looked over the parapet and exclaimed: 'There are our boys going over on the right,' These were C and D Companies. An officer of the Oxfords came along at the moment trying to straighten things out, but he had no detailed orders, and did not know where the flanks of the Companies were to rest. Moreover, there was no barrage.

Thus the three Companies went over most bravely, in face of almost certain failure. They had 250 yards of absolutely unfamiliar ground to cover. The rifle and machine-gun fire was intense, and terribly accurate. The Huns, having no shells directed at them, stood up in their trenches aiming deliberately at each man in the broken and thinning lines. Short rushes were made from shell-hole to shell-hole, each rush proving very costly in casualties. Few, if any, of the men got within 100 yards of the enemy. Captain Attride had been wounded in the body, and Captain Lewis in the thigh, and hardly an officer was left. It was evident that no bravery or determination on earth could turn failure into success. The men began, therefore, in accordance with orders to edge into a shallow communication trench only half finished, which the 5th Berks had started from their old line to 6th Avenue. It was a poor shelter, but offered a chance of safe return. Captain Lewis reached it with his orderly's help, and, though grievously wounded, was brought back. Captain Attride was shot through the head as he reached the very edge, and pitched forward dead. He had commanded D Company for nine months with the greatest tact and ability; his many friends mourned the best of comrades. Captain Blandy was shot through the face and blinded for the time while stepping out of the way of a wounded man lying at the bottom of the trench. Some men still lay out scattered in shell-holes, not daring to move, for the Hun still aimed at every living thing, picking off the wounded if they stirred. After a while a British aeroplane flew low over the scene, sounding its horn. Sergt. Page resourcefully lit some flares, which he had with him, and the pilot flew back. He proved a good friend in necessity, for almost immediately our 9.2's opened on 6th Avenue, the heads of the Huns disappeared, and the survivors made quickly for the communication trench. One of them, in entering, stepped on the body of an officer; he turned him over, and saw that it was Captain Attride. The casualties were naturally very heavy. Besides those officers already mentioned the killed were Lieut. O'Hara (1st East Surrey Regiment, attached), 2nd Lieut. Beasley (whose little son was presented with the M.M. which his father had won by the King when he visited Reading in March, 1918), and 2nd Lieut. Bartram, while 2nd Lieut. Taylor was wounded. He lay out for 48 hours, tended throughout that time with wonderful devotion by Sergt. Westall, who well earned a bar to his D.C.M. This sergeant, the bravest of the brave, when with the 2/4th next autumn near Arras, was last seen in a shell-hole close to the German wire, during a daylight patrol, laughing at the Huns, who were firing rifle grenades at him, but has since returned safely from captivity in Germany. Casualties among other ranks were 140, of whom 28 were killed and 31 missing, of most, if not all, of whom, I fear, no news has ever been heard. Failure is often more heroic than success, and I believe that those who read this imperfect account will realise that on August 14th the Battalion showed the highest and hardest form of courage.

As soon as the high ridge west of Pozières had been taken, a converging movement began upon Thiepval, that stubbornly defended height, which was not to fall until the 27th September. The 48th Division, facing half left, now began to move towards it from the south-east, whilst continuous pressure was directed from the west, or the direction of our old front line. On August 18th the 143rd (Warwick) Brigade attacked on a line about 1,000 yards north of Ovillers, with their right secured by a bombing attack made by B Company 4th Royal Berks. The ground round

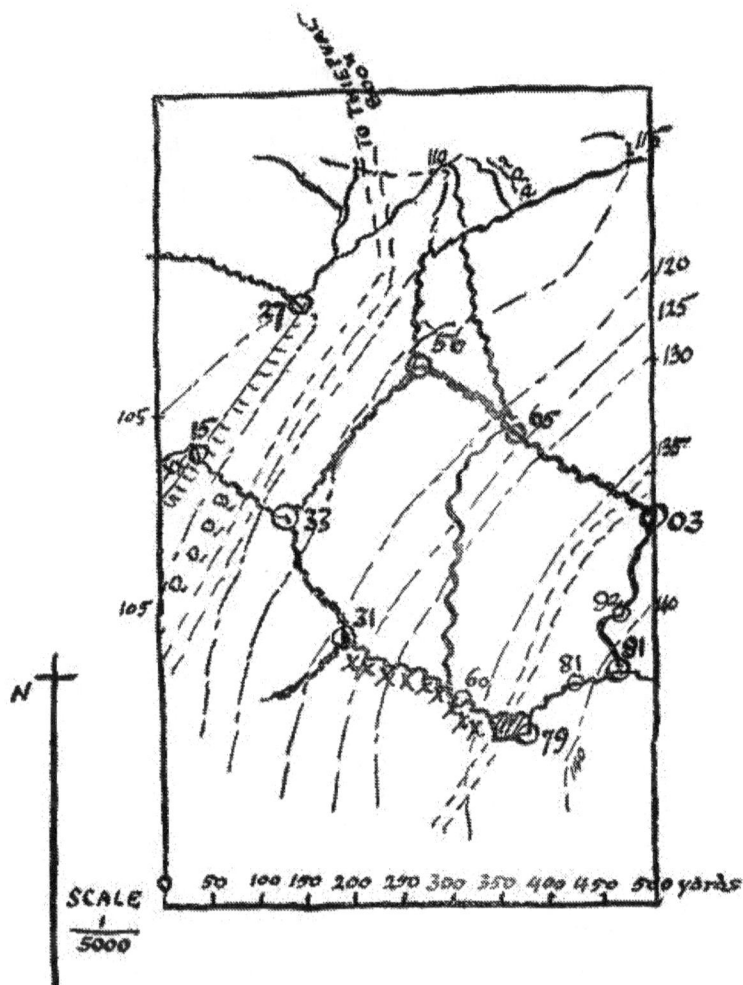

TO TREBAC &c.

110

115

120

115

130

105

105

37

56

65

15

33

103

135

31

92

140

81

91

60

79

N

SCALE
1
5000

0   50   100 150   200 250 300 350 400 450 500 yards

here was one of the grimmest of crater fields; almost every one of the many trenches which scarred it being marked on the map as either 'destroyed' or 'much damaged.' The 143rd Brigade attacked about 5 p.m. The whole course of the attack was visible to our men holding the front line, who looked over the parapet cheering and shouting with excitement as the successive waves moved inevitably forward and disappeared into the German trenches. Major Aldworth (O.C. B Company) handled his men with great skill, capturing 27 prisoners and a machine gun, and driving many of the enemy into the hands of the 6th Warwicks. Confused and fierce fighting went on until midnight; attack and counter-attack succeeding each other as either side received fresh supplies of men and bombs, but B Company finally held their objectives. The value of the bomb practice at Cramont was evident, for the men threw splendidly. Lieut. L. E. Ridley was killed fighting bravely at the head of his bombing party. Captains Cruttwell and Lacy, Lieuts. Wix and Smith (3rd East Surreys, attached), were wounded, the two former while getting their Companies ready for an expected counter-attack during the night. The remaining casualties amounted to nine killed and 36 wounded.

The fighting strength of the Battalion had now been reduced to about 500, but it was to take one last highly successful part in the Somme fighting before being withdrawn.

The Division had now reached a point about midway between Ovillers and Thiepval. A deep and narrow valley separated them from the latter stronghold, which rose steeply 170 feet above: a line of broken stumps standing forlornly near the crest line, 1,000 yards away, marked where the apple orchards had run along the southern outskirts of the little village. The enemy's positions lay astride this valley, thrust forward in a pronounced salient towards Ovillers. The whole of the Division were engaged in this attack, the

145th Brigade being in the centre, with 143 on the right and 144 on the left. The two assaulting Battalions of the 145th Brigade were 5th Gloucesters on the left and ourselves on the right. Each Battalion had a frontage of about 300 yards, our objectives being the point of the salient (79) and its eastern face, running obliquely across the hill slope towards the valley on the left (*i.e.*, from 79-92). The attack was launched at 5 p.m., heralded by a splendid barrage of three minutes' duration. More than 50 guns were firing on the Battalion's front alone, and their accuracy was perfect. The two Companies, A on the left, C on the right, moved up close behind the barrage, in which they showed complete confidence. On the right little difficulty was experienced, the trenches had been ruined, and many of their defenders buried. But the 8th Royal Warwicks, with whom our own men were to join hands in the trench running north from 92, were unable to reach their objectives, thus leaving an open flank. A strong point was therefore started at once in the heap of debris and scattered earth, known as Point 91, and a platoon of our old friends, 5th Royal Sussex, came up with the darkness and helped to dig a communication trench back to our old front line. No counter-attack developed, though shell-fire from the usual 5.9's was heavy for 12 hours, and the position was held securely until relief.

On the left there was more opposition. The key to the enemy's defence was Point 79: the trench here, and a collection of dugouts around it, had been almost untouched by our heavy guns. One of our platoons rushed up a communication trench leading from their assembly trench to Point 79, while two others kept pace along the open, one to the right and one to left. The enemy showed plenty of fight, standing on their parapets to throw bombs and to fire at the platoon advancing up the trench, in spite of cross-fire from Lewis guns, which did great execution amongst them.

They delayed, but could not check the advance, which broke through them into the disputed point. Lance-Corpl. Rixon, of Reading, deserves much of the credit for this success. He was in charge of the first bombing party in the communication trench. When they were held up, he sprang on the parapet, and from that point of vantage directed the bomb throwers, escaping unhurt himself by singular good fortune. This gallant action subsequently earned him the M.M. Unable to retire under cover, since the available trenches on either flank were already occupied, the Germans fled back across the open down the slopes of the hill, affording a target which was not neglected. Ten only remained to be taken alive, but their dead were thick on the captured ground. The 5th Gloucesters were already in their objectives, and the left flank was secured. A section of the R.E.'s following closely up helped to put the defences of 79 in order.

There were now, owing to casualties, no officers with A Company, but there was no lack of direction or control, thanks to Sergeant White, an old Territorial of many years standing. He inspired the men with his energy, and kept them constantly at work, moving up and down throughout the night under a rain of shells. He was rewarded with the D.C.M.

The attack had been well planned and well executed, and happily cost very little life. Thirty one men were killed or missing, and 50 wounded (including 2nd Lieuts. Garside and Buck). The men were specially pleased and proud of their success, which had been gained at the expense of the 5th Grenadier Battalion of the Prussian Guard. The latter had recently been sent to Thiepval after a commendatory speech from the Kaiser, which, as often, had failed to ensure good fortune. We were relieved next day by the 74th Brigade, and returned to bivouac at Bouzincourt. The 48th

Division, every unit of which had been engaged at least thrice, was to enjoy a well-earned rest. They received gratifying tributes to the value of the work achieved. The Army Commander wrote as follows: 'The Division has fought with only very short periods of rest since July 1st. Since then it has met and defeated many different units of the German Army, and has fully maintained the best traditions of British infantry. This record shows a high sense of discipline and honour in all ranks.' The Corps Commander (Lieut.-General Jacob) G.O.C., 2nd Corps, in forwarding his message to General Fanshawe, added his own tribute: 'Will you please express my gratitude and thanks to all the units under your command for their devotion to duty, and for the way they have fought and worked.... All ranks of artillery, engineers and infantry have carried out their tasks with such spirit and co-operation that the results have exceeded expectations. You have all done nobly and I congratulate you and your officers on the way the Division has worked. Your record in the recent operations is first rate.'

CHAPTER 12
Uneventful Days

The Battalion now moved back to Bus, that shady village with its white château so long used as Divisional Headquarters in the old days. Here General Fanshawe inspected the Battalion, addressed them on their late exploits, and presented Military Medals to Privates S. Smith and T. Russell. He spoke of the importance of practising open fighting, which he said might be the next task of the Battalion, a prophecy which, as we shall see, was fulfilled when we fought at Ronssoy in the German retreat next April. He added that the responsibility of officers and N.C.O.'s would be even greater than that in the late fighting, where all realised by experience how much depended upon them.

A short spell of 48 hours in the trenches followed in front of Auchonvillers, facing the coveted spur of Beaumont-Hamel, which was to fall in November. Here we sustained our only casualties during the month, one killed and one wounded, a happy contrast to August, when 286 men were put out of action. During this tour the Huns loosed a number of small balloons, which drifted behind our lines, scattering leaflets. These effusions, written in French for the benefit of the civil population, commented with brazen and comic impudence on the action of French aviators in bombing innocent German towns. The German military authorities, they amusingly remarked, believing that the French were incapable of such barbarity, thought that the airmen must have mistaken their objectives. But, no! The origin of these crimes is now known. They were expressly ordered by M. Poincaré, 'the slave of England.' (This new title for the President is printed in thick black type.) They are part of a devilish plan, conceived by England to revive the dying hatred of France against Germany, by forcing the latter Power to reprisals on French civilians, reprisals which she would be most reluctant to take. This illuminating specimen of German psychology deserves, I think, to be recorded.

The remainder of the month was divided between Beauval and Candas, a new village, whose inhabitants, with a curious naiveness, imagined that the blue hearts, which the Battalion wore as distinguishing badges, were the hallmark of a dangerous brand of storm-troops, and signified their desire to have the hearts of their enemies. So strong was this conviction among them that they locked their houses and refused us an entry until matters were explained. The barns allotted to the men were found half full of the produce of the harvest. The usual work was carried on; new drafts arrived steadily, men of good quality, but of little experience, though always with a leaven of old 1st/4th men returning after wounds and sickness. A number of new officers, 17 in all, also joined the Battalion from a variety of regiments, 5th Norfolks, 4th Northants, 4th Royal Sussex and 10th Middlesex, no supplies from our own Reserve Battalion being at the moment available. Further awards also of decorations won during July and August kept coming through with gratifying regularity, and will be found in the appendix. Finally the C.O. was awarded the D.S.O. to the delight of all ranks, who trusted him implicitly, knew how minutely he studied their comfort, and how much of their success was due to his untiring thoroughness in every detail of organisation.

October, that wettest of months, in which the last fires of the Somme flickered out, quenched by the everlasting rain, was spent by us in a variety of places, mainly well behind the lines, but far from comfortable. Such was Sombrin, 9 miles south-west of Arras, where officers were faced with the unpleasing alternative of sleeping in barns or in dripping and unboarded tents. Then we revisited Souastre after thirteen months, overlooking the ruins of Fonquevillers and the splintered remnants of Gommecourt Wood ravaged by 15-inch shells. Here again the liveliest activity was manifest. That successful finale to the year's fighting known as the Ancre Battle had been planned for October 14th, though owing to repeated postponements it was not launched until a month later. Again, day after day enormous working parties descended into Hébuterne, some to pursue mining operations under the R.E.'s, others to bury cable between the village and Sailly. Two strenuous days (12th and 13th) spent in the trenches immediately opposite Gommecourt cost us 16 casualties. Our line here still bore witness to the terrible bombardment which had frustrated the efforts of the 56th Division on July 1st, for long sections of trench then levelled and rendered impassable had not since been opened out. Every man not on duty was employed with one or other of the multifarious details for the expected attack, while on the morning of the 13th heavy shells were poured upon us, amongst them being many 11-inch. About this time Major Aldworth left the Battalion, to which he afterwards returned as Second-in-Command, to attend General Kentish's school for senior officers at Aldershot. B Company, as we have seen, did extraordinarily well under his command. The following

N.C.O.'s were promoted to commissioned rank at Souastre for bravery and good conduct in the field: Sergts. Wickens, Ross, Turner, Rogers, Cawley and Crust. The two latter gained command of B and A Companies respectively during 1918. These appointments were most gratifying to officers and men of the Battalion. During the remainder of the month we moved about from place to place in the neighbourhood of Beauval and between it and the Somme. It stands greatly to the credit of the Battalion's fitness and discipline that not a man fell out during all those marches in the rain over indescribably miry roads.

On October 31st an eastward move of the Brigade settled us in a camp at Millencourt, the village on the western hill looking down at Albert, on the fringe of the old battlefields. The fighting had died down, but an enemy had to be encountered more insidious and more trying to endurance and moral—namely, the mud and the cold.

CHAPTER 13

In the Slough of Despond

After three days at Millencourt the Battalion moved forward into that featureless waste for the possession of which so much blood had been shed. For 7 miles or more east of Albert along both sides of the great highway to Bapaume up the long slope from La Boisselle to Pozières windmill, and down again towards Le Sars, the eye would pick out no natural landmark except a few broken sticks, once trees. The surface of the country, churned up and scooped out by innumerable shells, was literally a sea of mud; where water had collected in the hollows it was deeply stained with green and yellow, the result of gas and fumes. The cold was coming, but at present was only sufficient to chill the mud through and through, not to freeze it into hardness. No buildings were available for the great army echelonned along this area, and few dugouts; the vast majority of all ranks lived out in rough shelters, or under the scanty protection of sodden tents. Though the infantry were glued to their shell-holes the artillery still maintained the characteristic activity of battle areas: and the few roads and paths available for transport and communication were their constant targets, especially during the hours of darkness.

The Battalion soon found that the hardships to be undergone far exceeded those experienced up to date. On their arrival at Lozenge Wood (so-called) they took over from the 11th Argyll & Sutherland Highlanders in the pouring rain a camp which consisted only of one bivouac sheet per platoon, and eight tents for officers: and any attempt at improvement was frustrated by the complete absence of material. Reserve and support lines were alike in affording no shelter of any kind, and the front trenches were naturally the worst of all, any part of which was considered to be in good condition if the liquid mud at the bottom did not exceed a foot in depth. No hot rations could be brought up, for the cookers could come no nearer than the ridge behind Martinpuich, more than 2 miles away as the crow flies. A 'Tommy's cooker' was served out to each section, but there were no dugouts in which to use it, and in the open the mud and rain were an effectual hindrance. The trenches themselves were in the shallow valley to the north of Le Sars, looking across to the last ridge that defended Bapaume, with Loupart Wood fringing its crest. On the left our line was extremely dangerous and weak, for it was enfiladed from the high ground in the direction of Pys; while the extreme left post in a chalkpit was not only isolated by 300 yards from the next Battalion, but had close by a covered ravine leading to the German lines. This post was, in fact, raided by the enemy soon after we had been relieved. This first tour lasted three days, and considering the violence and the methodical character of the shelling the Battalion were fortunate in having only 17 casualties. In addition five cases of trench feet were reported, for though dry socks were sent up every twenty-four hours, this could do little to mitigate hardship. It was rather surprising that the number of cases were so small, for amongst the men was a large draft of Yeomanry having their first experience of the trenches.

Meanwhile a new camp at Lower Wood, about a mile

behind Martinpuich, had been started, and we inhabited and improved it during the next four days. The rain had at last ceased; and the whole country was enveloped with those dense, clinging mists so characteristic of Artois, which at least had the merit of blinding the artillery's action.

On November 16th orders came for the Battalion to make an attack on the Butte of Warlencourt in 48 hours. Accordingly that night they moved up into the trenches on the east of the Bapaume road immediately facing the Butte. This ancient burial place rose steeply in a rounded hump 50 feet above the surrounding country about 500 yards north-east of Le Sars. Its greyish-white sides were pitted and scarred by shell-fire, but none the less in its chalky bowels it contained plenty of dugouts filled with machine gunners, who took full advantage of their dominant position. It had already been reached and even partially taken, but never held. The attack, however, was cancelled at the last moment. Everything, indeed, had combined to make success unlikely. The flanks were not secure, the weather was again thoroughly broken and the Battalion was very weak in numbers. Although the nominal ration strength was not much under 700, barely half of these were available for fighting purposes; in D Company at this time the average strength of platoons was only 13. In these wretched trenches the average casualties each day were about six, an apparently small number, perhaps, but equivalent in a year to twice the strength of a strong Battalion. The wastage from sickness was also high, while many of those who carried on in the line were tired almost to the point of collapse. Nor was there any rest, comfort or security in the camps behind. There were no fires, no cookhouses, only tents without floorboards. It was very different from the winter before, when, whatever the hardships of the line (and they were incomparably smaller) men could look forward to a good spell at Authie with its pleasant aspect, its untouched houses, its estaminets, and its cheerful civilian population. Almost the only thing which could now be done for the comfort of the men was the institution of a Battalion Canteen, at which all the articles bought from the Expeditionary Force Canteen were sold at cost price.

The weary interchange between camp and trench went on for nearly another month. Scotland and Chalk Trenches, the same line which had been taken over after first going forward from Lozenge Wood, were twice revisited. On the second occasion 2nd Lieut. Cawley was kept throughout in Destremont Farm with 20 men, and used entirely for patrol work. This new experiment proved a great success, for on one of these expeditions, which started from the chalk pit already mentioned on the left, they came by surprise on a German working party, and killed about 30 without loss to themselves. Among the many other troubles in these trenches was the exact knowledge which the Germans naturally possessed of their few dugouts, which the artillery firing (as always against captured ground) with great accuracy continually shelled. On December 8th C Company Headquarters were blown in and three casualties caused; next day a shell hit A Company Headquarters, with even more disastrous effect, killing 3 and wounding 6. These shelters might, it is true, be patched up, but with the earth liquefying all around and a shortage of material the result was not likely to be very secure. At last, on December 14th, the Battalion, now reduced in strength to 540 all ranks, moved back to Bécourt Camp, a mile south of La Boisselle. It was a poor place, but situated beyond the western border of the great waste, and practically immune from shell-fire. For the greater part of December the Battalion was commanded by Captain J. H. Goolden, who had returned during the Somme Battles after a long absence with the Brigade and Divisional Staff. Colonel Clarke was at this time on a month's leave in England, while Major Battcock had gone sick. Of the original officers who had gone out in March, 1915, there were now only four remaining: Colonel Clarke, Captains Goolden and Challoner, with the Quartermaster, Lieut. Payne. The interpreter, M. Hénaut, still remained with us, and indeed stayed on, always cheerful, willing and helpful, the friend of everybody, until our departure for Italy next November. The casualties (exclusive of sick) during this year of severe fighting amounted in all to 779, including 24 officers. As a result of these losses, and the impossibility of finding adequate local drafts, the Battalion during the latter half of the year gradually lost its exclusive Berkshire character, which at the beginning of the war had been its unique possession.

CHAPTER 14

The Winter and the German Retreat

Christmas was spent in the huts at Bécourt with a wild gale blowing; the festivities and feastings of the previous year at Authie were not possible, but at least the men could congratulate themselves that they were not in the trenches. On the 28th we moved back through Albert to the village of Bresle, which lies just north of the great straight highway from Amiens to Albert. Here some houses yet remained, and contact was re-established with the vestiges of civilisation. The Brigade, drawn up in a hollow square, was inspected by Lieut.-General Sir W. P. Pulteney, the Corps Commander, and earned his praise. Boxing competitions, concerts and football matches reappeared in the intervals of work. A train journey on January 9th took us to Citerne, a quiet, comfortable village, intact of war, in the French area south of the Somme. The inhabitants were most friendly, accommodation good, and each officer found a bed at his disposal. The three weeks' respite from the rigours of the line was the more appreciated as the great cold had now set in, which was to continue with almost unmitigated intensity until the middle of April. There was much to be done in the way of training, for the new platoon organisation had now come into force. Its object was to make the platoon a self-contained unit of specialists, with its four sections divided into riflemen, Lewis gunners, bombers and rifle-bombers. This was obviously to require from the average man a higher standard of specialisation than before, and consequently threw greater responsibility on the platoon and section commanders. It was, in fact, found impossible during the course of the 1917 campaign fully to attain this ideal, as the time available for the training of new drafts was not generally sufficient. Another train journey on January 28th took the Battalion by a circuitous route through Amiens, past Villars-Brettoneaux to Hamel, two names destined next year to become famous in the fighting history of the Australians. Hamel was soon exchanged for Cappy, a village high above the southern bank of the Somme, overlooking its great loops, and the widespread marshes and pools all frozen stiff. Although only about 2,000 yards behind the trenches from which the French started to the assault of Frise on July 1st, it was not badly knocked about. Houses and barns were available for billets, but the men suffered considerably from the cold, as fuel was very scarce, and the frost was now at its height, the thermometer marking 20 or more degrees of frost every night. Then followed a few days in the great French Adrian Huts, each holding a Company, in a camp by the edge of the Somme Canal a few hundred yards further east.

The month of February passed uneventfully, though unpleasantly, in alternatives between the trenches west of Peronne and Cappy. Until the 16th the extreme cold continued unabated, so that all the water which was brought up in petrol tins each night from Cappy froze solidly in transit. Another result of the severe weather more appreciated by the men was the hardness of the trenches, which made most of the ordinary trench fatigues impossible. A thaw, however, set in on the 16th, and a mist arose over all the country, which lasted for many days, and made it possible for the enemy to carry out unobserved his plans for the great retirement. Though further north throughout this very bitter weather fighting was incessant round Miraumont and the approaches of Bapaume, here inactivity prevailed, and the month cost the Battalion no more than nine casualties. There was also little sickness, and strength and fitness were well maintained.

March came in with a return of frost and snow, but the front was gradually waking into life. It was obviously the German policy to mask the moment of their withdrawal by lively activity, and their artillery and machine guns showed considerable vigour. On the other hand, though the British had not yet realised that the front was about to give along a stretch of 80 miles it was clear from the events round Bapaume that the enemy had for the first time begun to entertain the idea of ceding ground voluntarily. Hence raids for purposes of identification again became frequent. One of these was most successfully carried out by the Battalion on the night of 7th-8th March without any loss to themselves. The raiders were under the command of 2nd Lieut. Hampshire, and were divided into three small parties, each of 8 men. The portion of trench to be entered was shut off by a 'box barrage,' which, falling on both flanks and on the support line, enclosed it, so to speak, in a frame of shells. The wire was fully cut, and no difficulty was found in penetrating the enemy's line, but all the birds had flown beyond the limits of the barrages on either side. Accordingly, as no prisoner had been caught, a second attempt was made at 2.45 a.m. Again an entry was easily effected on the left; the party worked further down towards the south owing to the enlargement of the barrage, and finally found a small dugout, which was bombed. This had the effect of producing two Germans, who were carried off. The object of the raid thus happily accomplished, Hampshire and his men returned. The flanks throughout had been strongly held by the enemy, who fired rapidly but inaccurately, and caused no casualties whatever. The only effect of this action was to prevent the entry into their trench of our right-hand party towards La Maisonnette, which could not get through the hostile wire, but returned undamaged. The two prisoners were found, on examination, to belong to King Constantine's Own 88th Infantry Regiment, and had their shoulder-straps adorned with a crown and the letter K beneath. The G.O.C. of the Division sent special congratulations on the success of the whole operation. For their conspicuous share in this success, 2nd Lieut. Hampshire received the M.C., Sergt. A. C. Evans, Corpl. H. Hart, Lance-Corpls. J. Mazey and G. W. Hutchings the M.M.

Shortly after this the results of the weary and bloody months on the Somme battlefields became manifest. On March 17th-18th the enemy began his general retreat. The 48th Division was in the forefront of the pursuit south of the Somme. The 1st/7th Royal Warwicks were the first British troops to enter Peronne, and the flag which they planted on the ruined towers is now carefully preserved and treasured in the Imperial War Museum. Our Battalion was in reserve at Cappy practising Advance Guards. Open warfare was no longer relegated to the dim and uncertain future, but became the certainty of the moment. On the morning of the 20th operation orders were issued which began: 'The Battalion will move to Peronne at 11 a.m.' For the first time since they went abroad, they could advance unmolested over enemy country. The weather at last showed a delusive promise of spring, and the sun shone. Hopes ran high and all were pleased beyond measure to be leaving the mire and clay for the green untouched country beyond. They went over the forsaken trenches, crossed the

Somme by a bridge thrown over at Bézancourt Farm and entered Peronne. The little town, after its long history as a French fortress, after the battle of Mont St. Quentin and the German occupation of 1870, had now been laid utterly waste. Few houses had been previously damaged from shell-fire, since the French gunners had purposely spared the place, but now the destruction by the hand of the enemy was complete; it had been organised with the greatest care to make impossible military and civil occupation. In the suburbs the fruit trees had been felled; children's toys and all manner of debris, wantonly destroyed, lay about the streets. The Battalion was billeted in the remains of the barracks, and was joined during the evening and night by the rest of the Brigade.

Next day a march was made south-east along the Cologne Brook, which was crossed at Doignt. The roads were being everywhere busily repaired, the tall poplar trees which had been felled across them were being dragged out of the way, the great mine-craters at the crossroads were being filled up; the whole countryside was alive with labour repairing the damage for the advancing army. For some days the time was spent in outpost duty in the old style between Peronne and Roisel, and working on the defences which were being provisionally dug, till touch was fully restored with the Hun, and the limits of his retreat became clear. On March 24th the 5th Cavalry Division passed by, riding eastward, a sign of the new conditions of warfare. At Flamicourt, one of the adjacent villages used as billets for the Battalion for several days, were several interesting signs both of the carefulness of the enemy and of his hasty departure. In the street outside almost every house were great heaps of tin and zinc ready to be carted away; at another court was a pile of copper stripped from our shells. Here, too, for the first time was seen that inspiring yet most pitiful spectacle, a number of the civil population released from German captivity. The proof of victory, they were also an incitement to vengeance; their faces, from which all life and hope seemed to have departed, were a testimony to the misery which they had endured for the last 30 months. Among them were the inhabitants of Tincourt, whom the Germans, by a refinement of cruelty compelled to halt on the rise overlooking their homes and there to witness the destruction.

Meanwhile, in the bitter weather that had returned, incessant pressure was being exerted against the stubborn German rearguards, who were being gradually pushed eastward towards the much-vaunted defences of the Hindenburg Line.

CHAPTER 15

Ronssoy

The beginning of April found the 145th Brigade round Villers-Faucon in support to the other two Brigades who were fighting their way forward beyond Epéhy. On the 4th the Battalion received orders in concert with the remainder of the Brigade to take the three villages of Ronssoy, Basse Boulogne and Lempire. These three lie closely clustered together at the head of a valley with an undulating rise to the east. It was arranged to capture them by an encircling movement from the south and west. Snow fell heavily throughout the 4th, and frustrated all attempts of the Company Officers who had gone forward to see the lie of the land. A cold, dense mist wrapped everything in still greater obscurity when the Battalion moved off from Villers-Faucon at 2 a.m. The narrow sunken lanes, with numerous steep little hills, were clogged with snow. In spite of this we neither lost direction nor time, but reached the rendezvous at Templeux Wood by 4 a.m. Touch was obtained with the 8th Warwicks in Templeux village, who were prolonging the attack on the right, and with the 4th Oxfords on the left. The Companies were silently deployed a few hundred yards east of the wood. As the fighting was open and no elaborate defences were expected, each Company had a frontage of 200 yards, and was drawn up in depth with six waves each of two lines, the distance between the former being 50 yards and between the latter 25 yards. The village of Ronssoy was 1,600 yards away; between it and the attackers was a girdle of little woods, still untouched of green, and a number of small intersecting lanes and ditches. The enemy's outposts, as far as was known, were about 1,000 yards away, running north-west and south-east to cover the village. The morning was ideal for surprise, provided that mistakes were not made in the mist; for that reason no barrage would be provided unless called for by signal rockets.

We must now follow the fortunes of the three Companies, who began their advance at 4.30 a.m. B Company, on the right, had only gone 200 yards before enfilade fire was directed at them through the darkness from the slag-heaps on the right. A platoon was detached to deal with it, and its garrison, fearing encirclement, gave themselves up to the 8th Worcesters, who were coming up on the other side. Another 800 yards advance disclosed a further obstacle: the wire of the German outposts with well-manned trenches just behind. A Lewis gun was brought into action, gaps were cut, a barrage called for, which descended on the enemy at 5.45 and shortly afterwards the position was gained without any hand-to-hand fighting. The Company now turned to its fourth task of protecting the flank of the Battalion, and dug themselves in on a line just east of the captured slag-heap. A Company under Captain Challoner, in the centre, also ran into the wire of the same position rather further north, but were able to break through without much difficulty. Then, led by Captain Challoner with great dash and determination, they pushed on rapidly through the eastern outskirts of the village, seized the cemetery, and there divided. One platoon joined hands with the 7th Gloucesters, whose successful attack from the west had put them in possession of the joint hamlets of Lempire and Basse Boulogne. The remainder, moving to the right, occupied a bank 800 yards south-east of the village, which had been designated beforehand as the left of the new outpost position. This long advance of 1-1/2 miles over unknown country with the successful division of forces just after the assault, when disorganisation is most wont to occur, reflects the highest credit on all concerned. Captain Challoner, who kept the firmest grasp throughout, and both inspired and controlled his men, well deserved the Military Cross which was awarded a few days later. A fine example of initiative was shown by Sergt. Millican, whose Platoon Commander was killed as the village was entered: taking charge instantly he led his men with distinction throughout the rest of the fight.

To D Company on the left fell the lion's share of the fighting and of the booty. Approaching unobserved almost to the south entrance to the village, they overwhelmed two hostile posts in the first light of dawn, killing every man among them and taking two machine guns. Though their flank was for the moment open, as the Oxfords were held up on the edge of Ronssoy Wood, they burst into the village. Here was the wildest confusion. No attack had been expected in the wild weather, and the enemy were in their cellars and dugouts just sitting down to breakfast. Figures could be seen running about outlined in the snow; at a corner of the street a sergeant-major was shouting and beckoning to his men to fall in round him. D Company, wild with excitement, hunted them through the cellars and lanes and made a great slaughter. The dead lay all about the streets and in the bombed dugouts. Lieut. Rogers, O.C. No. 16 Platoon, was reputed to have killed eight himself. Those Huns who escaped ran pell-mell singly or in groups up the hill and along the Hargicourt road, flinging away their packs, with which the slope was littered. Captain James, who had led the Company so gallantly and successfully, got them together and wheeled round to the east of the village in the chance of exploiting still further the result achieved. Through the clearing mist a battery could be dimly seen on the ridge 1,000 yards away limbering up and then disappearing over the crest, and it seemed possible to advance there, and thus command a view into Hargicourt. Unfortunately at this moment our barrage, by some unexplained mistake, fell upon the eastern exit of the village, causing several casualties. Part of the Company, therefore, made its way to its alloted position in the outpost line. The remainder cleared up Ronssoy, and found all kinds of booty. Soup, coffee, bread and sausages were all ready in the dugouts and were consumed by the victors. A mail had just come in, and the letters lay about unopened. The equipment and packs were examined with keen interest. Everything was new and of the best material, for the Huns had just come from Russia, and had been hastily fitted out for the Western Front. In every pack, in addition to the usual articles, were a change of underclothing and three pairs of socks. One fortunate sergeant found a bottle of whisky in a dugout, which was quickly shared; it was not till afterwards that he discovered that it was not legitimate loot, but the property of the Brigade M.G. officer, who had appropriated the dugout and most incautiously left unguarded his treasure, which he had brought up with him in the attack. At the other end of the village a lively dispute was going on with the Oxfords, who were found carrying off the two machine guns captured when the outposts were rushed. The men were wonderfully excited and delighted at their achievement, and have always declared since that it was the best fight they have ever had in France.

The enemy's artillery had been active throughout the attack, but ineffective, as it was without direction. It had shelled

LIEUT.-COL. A. B. LLOYD-BAKER, D.S.O., T.D.
COMMANDING FROM 13 APRIL, 1918 TO 1 SEPTEMBER, 1918

Brigade Headquarters and the ground in front of Templeux Wood, but had never overtaken the attack. Throughout the day 5.9-inch shells were poured into Ronssoy, but did no damage whatever, as the men were either in the unlocated outpost line, or withdrawn well west of the village. A patrol of C Company managed during the day to get up to the ridge and look into Hargicourt, in front of which the enemy were visible, digging actively. Once or twice small patrols of Uhlans rode along the skyline, the first enemy cavalry that had yet been seen. No counter-attack of any description was attempted, and it was clear that the enemy rearguards, who were not in great strength, had been seriously inconvenienced by this surprise capture of their positions. General Fanshawe, who, as usual, was not far behind, soon came up, and after going over the village said he had not seen a better day's work since he had been in France.

The casualties in officers were heavy, which is explained by their conspicuous gallantry in leading and directing their commands over the unfamiliar country. Four were killed or died of wounds; 2nd Lieuts. Garside, Heppell, Hunt and Bostock; while Captain James and 2nd Lieut. Rogers were wounded. Other ranks escaped very lightly with 9 killed and 39 wounded.

CHAPTER 16

Towards the Hindenburg Line

April pursued its bitter way with snow and sleet. The first and triumphant stage of the Battle of Arras was fought on the 9th, when the enemy was thrust back 5 miles with the heaviest losses in prisoners and guns which he had yet suffered at the hands of the British. The repercussion of this violent fighting was felt all along the British line, and particularly to the southward, where the positions were still semi-fluid. The enemy's object was to delay as long as possible in his outposts before the Hindenburg Line, while the British endeavoured to push him rapidly upon his main positions, which would then be open to regular attack. Accordingly, small actions to seize local tactical features were epidemic throughout the 4th Army during this month. The Battalion at first rested from its labours in the village of Hamel, its former halting place in January, from 5th to 13th April, when it returned via Villers-Faucon to take over from the Oxfords. The line had by now been consolidated some 2,000 yards east of Ronssoy on the slopes of the hill, the crest of which was occupied by the German outposts, the key to whose position was the fortified farm of Guillemont. The Battalion was ordered to attack this point next evening in conjunction with a combined night movement by the whole Division. The weather was again vile, and wet snow fell incessantly. The night was pitch dark, and without firing lights it was impossible to see 5 yards. The attack was due to start at 11.30 p.m. It was to be carried out by two Companies, C and D. The password was 'Wilson,' which called to mind the entry of the United States into the war a few days previously. The Companies arrived punctually after a march of 2 miles from support, and began to form up for the assault. While they were doing so, covering parties ahead reported that the enemy were advancing on the right flank. This was probably a patrol, but Captain James wisely pushed forward a platoon of D Company to secure his Company's advance. The enemy disappeared into the darkness, and immediately telephoned to their artillery, which promptly put a heavy and accurate barrage on our men who were formed up on open ground with no kind of cover. This caused 30 casualties, and as the men were so cold that they could hardly hold, much less fire, their rifles, it was decided not to proceed with the attack, and they were withdrawn to the trenches. A second attack, which was proposed for 1.30 a.m., was vetoed by the Brigade. General Fanshawe, when addressing the Battalion on the 22nd April, said that he was 'fully satisfied with the effort put forward, and that if it had been possible to reach the objective the Battalion would have done so.' Guillemont Farm was taken by the 144th Brigade on 24th April. In this attack our Battalion cooperated after a few days' renewed rest at Hamel, where the immediate awards to officers and men for the fight at Ronssoy were made.

The attack, on the night of the 24th-25th resolved itself, as far as the Battalion went, into a demonstration. Apparently owing to the darkness of the night and the width of frontage allotted to the attacking Companies, touch was lost with the right Battalion of the 144th Brigade which was enveloping Guillemont Farm from the south. As our rôle was to protect the right flank, and as the attack on the left was disorganised by shell-fire, the operations came to a standstill. Dawn arrived before it was possible to sort out the attackers and to get a fresh Company into position. The two Companies engaged, A and B, lost only 1 killed and 9 wounded from machine gun fire. The net result of the attack was that Guillemont Farm was taken, but the Quennemont Spur to the south remained in the enemy's hand. The Battalion next day took over the whole of the front concerned from Companies of each of the four Battalions of the 144th Brigade. The relief was long and laborious, as all the Companies were mixed together and their exact limits uncertain. The enemy, expecting a renewal of the attack, showed great nervousness, and put down a counter-preparation three times during the night, but without doing much harm. This state of anxious expectancy continued during the remainder of the tour making life the more unpleasant, as the trenches were as yet improvised, and supplies had to be brought up over the open. Much patrolling was done to discover the exact position of the enemy's forward posts, while the snipers of D Company from their commanding position in Guillemont Farm claimed several victims. At sunset on the 29th the 7th Worcesters relieved us, and we went back into billets at Villers-Faucon. The long winter had ended, and spring arrived with a burst of sun and warmth. A fortnight's well-earned rest was now to follow, in which time could be given to refit and to assimilate the new drafts, which, however, were only sufficient to bring the total strength, from 600 to 700 men. It was remarked that although the general quality was good, out of the first contingent of 35, five wore trusses and three others possessed flat feet, varicose veins or hammer toes.

CHAPTER 17

The Renewal of Trench Warfare

The great attempts to break through in April had definitely failed from a variety of causes. The Russian Revolution had rendered impossible the blow in the East, for which British munitions had for the first time adequately armed the Russian Armies. The German retreat had partially disorganised the combined British and French plan. The failure of Nivelle's great blow at the Chemin des Dames on the 16th April with enormous losses, made the French Armies incapable of any offensive operation on a large scale for several months. Hence the Battle of Arras, which had begun so happily, degenerated towards the end of April into a series of furious struggles, each of which showed less promise of decisive importance than the last. The centre of gravity shifted to the north, where preparations on a vast scale were pushed forward for the main attack in Flanders, which opened on 31st July. Accordingly, the southern sector in which the Battalion remained, settled down into a normal period of what is called inactivity.

The Battalion spent the beginning of May in the ruins of the village of Doignt, now greatly improved since they passed over the blasted roads on the 22nd March. Here the time passed in the usual training and recreations, and a Challenge Cup, presented by the C.O., was competed for in inter-Platoon Football Matches. Here, too, an invaluable thresher installed at Peronne disinfected the blankets, which were in a filthy condition. On the 12th the Battalion, now under Major Aldworth's command, as the C.O. was Acting Brigadier, moved to Combles, and entered the 15th Corps area. The old Corps Commander rode up to the Brigade on the way and expressed his regret at leaving such a gallant and well-behaved Brigade. The old Somme battlefields were still entirely desolate, the ground was full of corruption and noxious fumes and littered with the debris of battle. Far away, on the eastern horizon, a green strip appeared, showing the limits of the devastation. Next day the march was continued through the centre of the waste past Le Transloy to a capacious camp at Beulencourt on the Peronne road, 2 miles south of Bapaume. Next day the Battalion re-entered the line in front of Hermies, relieving the 9th Sherwoods, whose C.O., Colonel Thornton, came from our 1st Battalion. Until the end of June our lot was cast in this neighbourhood with normal periods of trench duty and relief. The line held by the Brigade stretched south from the great Bapaume-Cambrai road. It was from these trenches that the northern part of the surprise attack against Cambrai was launched on 20th November. The enemy was ensconced in his Hindenburg Line, which took advantage of every undulation in the bare tableland. The villages in our occupation, Hermies, Doignies and Beaumetz, had all shared in the systematic devastation of the spring. The foremost British line was still a matter of partially connected outposts, each Platoon forming as a rule a self-contained strong point, while inter-communication with other posts was always difficult and sometimes impossible by day. The Battalion frontage was strung out to a width of about 2,300 yards, and on our arrival was protected only by discontinuous belts of wire, but before the first tour had been completed they had all been linked together. No Man's Land was wide and ill-defined, amounting sometimes to 1,000 yards, with such debateable features as ruined farms or clumps of trees situated in the midst, which required constant patrolling, but were found regularly unoccupied. The aspect of the country with its tangled growth of grass and weeds revived memories of Hébuterne two summers ago.

Thus six weeks were spent in comparative stagnation. Again the enemy's artillery were almost silent for days on end, though now and again violent bursts of 5.9-inch would be directed at the Support Companies. The Battalion made no raids; the only one which was attempted against them was on a small scale, and was completely crushed by Sergeant Garrett, of Wokingham, whose good leadership of the post attacked earned him the Military Medal. We suffered no loss, and took one prisoner entangled in the wire. The total casualties for the period were no more than 15, but included Captain Down, who died of wounds on 22nd May. He had been with the Battalion since the spring of 1916, and was deeply regretted as a capable officer, who showed always the greatest consideration for his men. On 30th June the Battalion turned their backs on this quiet spot and marched by stages through Velu and Bihucourt northwards to Bailleulval, a village about 6 miles southwest of Arras, now 10 miles behind the line to which it had been in close proximity until that spring.

Here every sign suggested that the Battalion was soon to take part in an offensive. Drafts arrived in such numbers that the total strength was raised to 930, a higher figure than at any period since we first crossed to France. Training went on feverishly through the sultry days. The old system of trenches in front of the village were the scene of many practice attacks, nor did the musketry, bombing, and gas specialists neglect their opportunities. The Brigadier appeared, to give lectures and to inspect the capacity of each officer to use his compass. The Divisional General carried off all the senior officers for staff rides. Thus the three weeks were spent in most arduous preparation, which left no doubt that a severe ordeal was imminent. That a general offensive was intended in the north was no secret either to our Army or to the enemy, and was indeed the natural sequel to the Battle of Messines. All doubts were resolved when the Battalion entrained on 21st July at Mondicourt and moved north into Flanders. They passed along the same route by which exactly two years before they had come down to Hébuterne, and the survivors of those days cheered as they passed the well-remembered little towns of Marles and Lapugnoy. As the evening drew in the train wandered slowly through Lillers and Hazebrouck, vast centres of activity, finally drawing up at Godewaersvelde at 10.45 p.m., whence a weary march ended at dawn at Houtkerque, which, curiously enough, was next door to our first resting place in Flanders,—Winnezeele. The entire move had occupied 20 hours; it is interesting to note that while the direct distance between the two points was 43 miles, the Battalion had traversed by road and rail at least 70.

CHAPTER 18

The Third Battle of Ypres

The prolonged and terrible struggle which was now about to begin was the last attempt to break through in the west on the old plan. The immense collection of guns, ammunition, railway material, and every kind of transport aroused high hopes. It was believed that the bombardment prolonged throughout many days with an intensity far greater than before the Somme would overwhelm the German resistance, and open the way to the Flanders coast and to the submarine bases then at the most successful height of their activity. These expectations were disappointed. The German positions no longer consisted of continuous trench lines, which could be reduced to shapeless masses of earth. An organisation of great depth had taken their place. Machine gun nests and pill-boxes scattered about were almost indistinguishable from the sea of mud in which they were placed, and defied accurate aerial reconnaissance. In this fortified zone the foremost lines were weakly held, and the British troops after taking them found the main resistance still before them, when their energies were almost exhausted by their painful journey through the mire. The artillery had done its work only too well in tearing the soil to pieces; but had none the less left intact many a pill-box which would only succumb to the direct hit of a 9.2-inch shell. The dice of success were thus loaded heavily against the attackers, and complete victory was rendered impossible by the incredible weather. The great storm which raged throughout the initial attack on July 31st was succeeded by almost unprecedented rain throughout August. The brief improvement of September relapsed into the deluges which made the last stages of the struggle for Passchendaele so heroic a feat of endurance. The last month of the Somme Battle had been terrible, but the whole of the events now to be described were fought under far worse conditions. No trenches or dugouts were available for sheltering the troops in the battle area, of whom only a small fraction could be accommodated in such pill-boxes as remained intact. The corduroy paths by which alone rations and stores could be brought up were gassed and shelled night and day; one false step was to be engulfed sometimes beyond hope of recovery. The artillery were in little better case, their guns were placed almost wheel to wheel in the open, always sinking deeper into the morass, and unable to move away from the storm of shells. The light railways on which they depended for a regular supply of shells often sank themselves from lack of solid foundation. Far behind, junctions, dumps and rest camps were attacked by long-range fire and bombs, with a violent persistency quite unprecedented until the March days next year. The ordeal was bitterly hard, and the prize incompletely won, but the spirit of the British Armies rose supreme over all, and the German defence was taxed to the uttermost.

The 31st July brought the Battalion no excitements. Leaving camp soon after midnight they crossed the Belgian frontier and moved to St. Jan Ter Beezen, just west of Poperinghe. The flickers and rumble of the greatest bombardment yet known in war accompanied them through the night. The rain descended and the floods came for the next three days. Again, as in the days of Loos and the Somme, the first expectations and the eager hopes were disappointed. Success had been only partial; the weather was impossible, operations were postponed. Next day the sodden men found themselves in dripping tents, just pitched, a stage nearer the line at Dambre Farm, in the low country west of Ypres. On the 5th the battlefield was reached. All through the afternoon at five minutes' interval the platoons moved up. Heavy shells followed them all the way. At dusk the relief of the 188th Brigade in the reserve lines south of St. Julien was completed. Water stood everywhere, the trenches were blotted out, the pill-boxes themselves were flooded. The shelling was incessant, and no sleep was possible that night. On the night of the 6th-7th the 1st/4th Oxfords were relieved, and 24 hours were spent on either side of St. Julien through which runs the Steenbeck, foulest of streams. Next night, amidst violent thunder, the Battalion crawled back to Dambre Camp. The four days had cost them 11 killed and 31 wounded, which might well have been increased but for the steady discipline prevailing among all ranks.

Next week the attack, whose date was yet unknown, was sedulously practised in all its details. A large scale model of the ground was inspected by all officers and N.C.O.'s at Divisional Headquarters. On the 15th the time for action had arrived. The march to the battle was slow and deliberate. The men halted at midday at the camp of Reigersberg, ate and slept. Then ate again a last hot meal before setting out on their final journey through the darkness. All the Companies were in position by 3.30 a.m. on the 16th. Then followed a period of anxious inactivity, until at 4.45 the British barrage burst forth in its awful salute to the dawn. Men began to advance against the enemy on the whole front of 25 miles; the second act of the great struggle had begun.

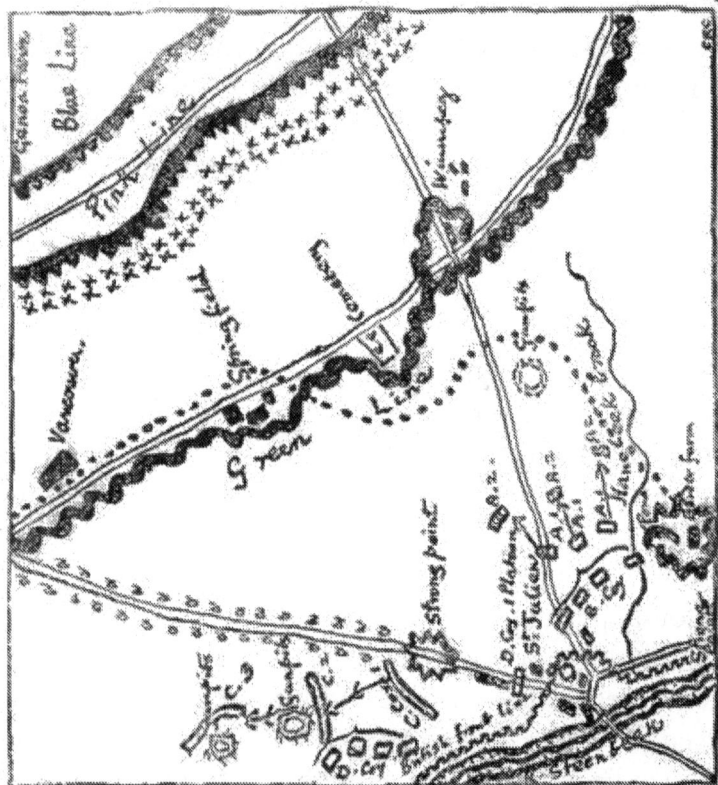

Canadian Farm
Blue Line
Pink Line
Wieltje
Canal
Spay field
Vancouver
Green
Strong point
D.Coy & Platoon "B" Coy
A.Coy
St Julien
Gun pits
Doxy
Fortuin Cross Roads
Mouse Farm
Red Farm
O. Coy
Black Line
Green Line

N

500 yds

The attack was, on the whole, a complete failure, though on the left the French made progress through the swamps towards Houthulst Forest, and the 23rd Division took Langemarck. In the centre, where our Division was engaged, progress was infinitesimal. The enemy troops, hidden in their deep and inconspicuous labyrinth of defence, were fresh and fought stoutly. Our attack was based on the support of tanks, which, owing to the condition of the ground, could not come into action. The forces alloted were far too weak to approach the ambitious objectives which had been assigned to them: and were fortunate if they succeeded in winning a few hundred yards after a long and desperate struggle which left them crippled. Our Battalion had a hard and disspiriting task. Assigned as Reserve to the Brigade it had been intended to sweep through the assaulting Battalions to the final objective. Actually their rôle was reduced to hanging about under violent shelling, almost stationary, turning now to right, now to left, to fill up gaps in the line, or to ward off threatened counter-attacks, always waiting for an order to advance which never came.

Although I have avoided criticism as far as possible in this narrative, I cannot refrain from saying, after a careful study of the documents available, that the staff work of the 5th Army (General Gough) was thoroughly bad as far as our Division was concerned. Time after time units were set impossible tasks, with inadequate support from artillery and tanks, and with ludicrously small reserves. This opinion is thoroughly shared by others more competent to pass judgment than myself.

The order of battle for the Brigade was as follows:— Starting from the line of the Steenbeek the three Battalions, covering a frontage of about 1,200 yards, were to take the fortified line of the Langemarck road from the crossroads at Winnipeg to those just west of Keerselare. This accomplished, their assault was to take them beyond the Pink and Blue lines to an outpost position along the farms of Flora Hubner and Stroppe. The 5th Gloucesters on the right joined the Ulster Division, the Bucks Battalion was in the centre, and on the left the 4th Oxfords touched the 12th Division. It will thus be seen that the Brigade, unsupported, was expected to advance about a mile through the mud, everywhere ankle-deep, taking on its way three regularly-organised positions, to say nothing of the intermediate strong points with which the ground bristled. The enemy was at his strongest, well-prepared and expectant. The 7th Bavarian Regiment, which faced us, had just come into line; it was part of a good Division, the 5th Bavarian. His barrage descended only three minutes after our own had begun. It is not surprising that, as a result, no impression was made even on the line of the Langemarck road, except at one point round Springfield. The fight swayed about round the pill-boxes, disused gun-pits and fortified farms which studded the countryside. Each one of these had to be taken separately; the pill-boxes in particular had to be rushed by bombers, who crept up and threw their bombs through the loopholes, which meanwhile were silenced by continuous machine-gun fire. One of these structures, entirely surrounded by water except for a narrow causeway, successfully defied all attempts at capture.

Meanwhile, our four Companies had varied experiences just behind this all-day battle. A Company on the right, advancing over the Steenbeek at zero, caught the full blast of the barrage. Captain Tripp (3rd East Surreys), who was in command, was immediately killed, and the only other officer, 2nd Lieut. Brooke, wounded. 2nd Lieut. Buck was then sent from Headquarters to take command. During the remainder of the day the Company, harassed continuously by shells and rifle fire (for the enemy held positions within

300 yards of them), reduced in strength by almost a half, succeeded in maintaining touch with the Ulsters and the Gloucesters. Twice the enemy, pushing forward small parties, tried to find a gap, but was arrested at once. The line remained, curving in an arc east of St. Julien, about 200 yards beyond the starting point. B Company also experienced great difficulty in making their way through the barrage. Captain Norrish, who was in command, walked up and down looking for a gap. After a while he brought them through by the north-east corner of St. Julien. Thence, turning right-handed in small parties, they dug in behind A Company and the Gloucesters. For the remainder of the day they remained in support to the latter, who were vainly endeavouring to force their way forward to the Lange-marck road. This Company seems to have lost about 40 men during the day. To C Company fell such small share of actual fighting as came the way of the Battalion. The Bucks, on moving forward, were held up by a large strong point at Hillock Farm, which resisted obstinately with machine guns. Two platoons of C Company, creeping up from the north-west, played their Lewis guns upon the loopholes. The farm was encircled and taken, 50 of the garrison were killed and the remainder captured. This was about 7 a.m. During the next three hours the Bucks thrust slowly forward, losing heavily all the way. By 10.30 they had gained a precarious footing in the Green line on a front of about 200 yards round Springfield. Their position was very dangerous, as both their flanks were in the air. The Oxfords, on their left, had been completely hung up, and were barely beyond our front line. Two platoons of C Company pushed up northwards into the gap at 11.30, but found only small parties of the enemy, who enfiladed them at close range from some disused gun-pits 200 yards west of the Poel-capelle road. These snipers caused constant casualties, and

when Captain Holmes was hit at noon all the officers had been put out of action. Under the leadership of Sergt.-Major Heath they cleared the gun-pits and extracted six prisoners, the only trophies of the day; there they remained until relief, losing at least 50 men. C.S.-M. Heath obtained the M.C. D Company, contrary to their experience at Ronssoy, had the easiest time of the four. Held back on the western bank of the Steenbeek by the congestion at the bridges until 5.15 a.m., they crossed when the barrage, always lighter on our left, had greatly slackened and suffered only slight loss. They dug in near the eastern bank, and remained all day there in support of the Bucks. At noon one platoon moved forward to the right, and securing the Bucks' right flank, kept in connection with the posts of A Company. The losses of this company were about 30 men. In all the casualties of the Battalion were 35 killed (including Captain Tripp), and 138 wounded and missing (including Captains Winslow and Holmes and 2nd Lieuts. Brooke, Oldridge and Wood). This amounted to about a third of the fighting strength. The remainder of the Brigade suffered more heavily, especially the Bucks, who had clung for hours with splendid gallantry to the exposed and practically untenable position round Springfield.

The Battalion next day was relieved by Companies at dawn and dusk, and reassembled at Dambre Camp. The respite was short, for before many days the Division was called again to make a fresh attempt at the same spot. Although no general attack was found practicable until the 20th September, it was apparently deemed essential first to gain a footing on the low ridge of Gravenstal, which, though it rose only 60 feet above the Steenbeek Valley, dominated the country as far as Ypres, and gave the enemy eyes to see our preparations. The next attack was fixed for 27th August; this time it was the turn of the 143rd and 144th Brigades to attack, while we remained in Divisional Reserve. The front and the objectives were almost exactly the same. On the left was the 11th Division, on the right the 61st, our second line. It was the first time that these two had come together on the battlefield, and the occasion was not fortunate, for both were unable to make headway and lost severely. The plan of attack showed great lack of imagination, and shook general confidence in the staff of the 5th Army. The lessons of the 16th seemed to have been entirely thrown away. The same impossible advance was expected. The ground was far worse than before. The water lay knee-deep in the valley. As the men struggled forward they could be seen pulling one another out of the glutinous mud in which they had sunk to the waist. The tanks, promised as before, were unable to perform. Finally, the attack started at the singular hour of 1.55 p.m., which rendered concealment of all the final preparations impossible, and gave the German machine gunners deadly opportunities for dealing with the reserves who poured up in the afternoon along the crowded tracks. The Battalion arrived at its assembly place on the road running through St. Julien about 3.30 p.m., and, as before, waited on events. Towards dusk it became known that the Warwicks' attack had completely failed, while further north the 7th and 8th Worcesters succeeded after four hours' fighting in seizing the Green line from Springfield as far as the Keerselare cross roads. At 8 p.m. all hope of a further advance in the Warwick area had gone, and the Battalion was ordered to relieve the shattered Brigade, one Company taking the place of each Battalion. There was naturally much difficulty in taking over, and next morning it was discovered that three platoons of the 8th Warwicks, whose position was unknown to their C.O., were still lying unrelieved round Border Farm. Meanwhile, on the evening of the 27th, confused fighting still went on north of Springfield, where the

1st/4th Oxfords had been brought up to try by exploiting the success already gained to turn the Spot Farm-Winnipeg portion of the Green line. No further ground, however, was secured; the men were at the limits of their endurance, and by next morning it was clear that everything had combined to render a further attack impossible. The day was therefore, passed quietly for the exhausted combatants; in front the stretcher-bearers bravely and indefatigably picked up the wounded, who had lain out all night in the liquid mud. That night two companies of the 2nd/10th London relieved us. Thus half a Battalion held defensively the whole fighting front of a Brigade. We returned again to Dambre Camp, which the enemy shelled viciously with a naval gun. The Battalion may be considered fortunate in losing only 11 killed (including Captain Norrish, 10th Middlesex), and 51 wounded (including Captain Shaw, 4th Northants).

St. Jan Ter Beezen now reharboured the Battalion, which was built up again in strength by a succession of curious little drafts of 6 and 11. The usual training, increasing in intensity as the men recovered from the fatigue of battle, was carried on through a spell of close and thundery weather. The nights were more than once disturbed by a shower of bombs. On 16th September a train journey removed us far from the front to Audenfort, near Calais, to occupy the farms and barns of several scattered hamlets. The attitude of the population, as sometimes happened in the back areas, was unfriendly. The reason, doubtless, is that the distance from the realities of war is apt to make the inhabitants less accommodating and the troops less well-disciplined. In this case, however, excellent relations were established in a few days. The training during the ensuing ten days was mainly confined to musketry, and A Company had the satisfaction of beating all the other companies of the Division in a field practice fired under the eyes of the G.O.C.

On the 27th September the Battalion returned to the same blighted region, now enveloped by dense autumn mists. The great attack of 20th September had rolled forward the tide of battle for more than a mile, and the British, now ensconced in the demolished farms on the east side of the Gravenstal Ridge, were preparing to carry out another stage of that painful and bloody progress. At dawn on 4th October the 143rd Brigade attacked through us, advancing some 1,500 yards. The Battalion spent the next three days in an uneasy reserve, changing their quarters every 24 hours, continuously soaked by the rain, which again fell pitilessly. On 7th October they regained the front line, pulling one another out of the trackless mire as they crawled up through the dripping night, plentifully sprinkled with gas on their way. Next night was even worse; the 7th Worcesters came up to relieve us under shell-fire; most of the guides we sent down to them were either killed or buried and the relief was long and arduous. The 144th Brigade attacked again on the 8th-9th October, under the worst possible conditions; our Battalion, in Divisional Reserve, was allotted to the Brigade, and lay out scattered by Companies until dusk on the 9th, ready to repel counter-attacks and to lend help as required, but was not actively engaged. The total casualties during this period amounted to 84, of whom 16 were killed. All who took part in these ten days' operations agree that the hardships suffered by the men exceeded everything yet endured on active service. The exhausted troops were taken back to Dambre Camp on the 9th by motor lorries. This was their last experience of that tremendous and ill-conducted battle, in which they had been engaged with but slight intermission for 70 days.

CHAPTER 19

Last Days in France and
the Journey to Italy

On 15th October the Battalion left the Flemish swamps
for good, and, returning south by rail, eventually settled for
the remainder of the month in the huts at Villars-au-Bois,
north-west of Arras. Here they rested in pleasant country
behind the 2nd Canadian Division, one of whose regiments, the 27th, they replaced in reserve. The former were
a splendid body of men, and very friendly. Their Quartermaster excited general admiration, being a man of over 60
years of age, two of whose sons were serving in the same
Battalion as Second-in-Command and Adjutant. As usual,
after active operations adequate drafts arrived of both officers and men; the former came mainly from the 3rd Wilts,
the latter from the M.T., who, though practically ignorant
of infantry work, soon developed in a very satisfactory
way. From 2nd-10th November we occupied the sector
in front of Vimy Ridge, the scene of the great Canadian
victories in April, looking across to the devastated mining
town of Lens. The Canadians had done all that was possible to improve the trenches, which the counter-bombard-
ment of either side had levelled, and they were generally
good except on the left, where all the soil had been shot
away. The dugouts, as generally in ground captured from

the Huns, were excellent; there was little fighting activity, and no more than three casualties were suffered. On the 8th the Battalion received the thanks of the 31st Division for their assistance in a daylight raid carried out by the latter on our right. Smoke-clouds were emitted from our trenches, while the skilful manipulation of life-sized dummies successfully produced the illusion of lines of men issuing from their trenches, who drew on their wooden bodies the desired effect of heavy enemy fire. On November 14th Savy and Villars Brulin received the Battalion. These little villages, some 12 miles from the firing line near the source of the Scarpe, were, though we knew it not, to be the last billets of the Battalion in France. Every autumn the enemy had replied to our offensive in France with a furious blow elsewhere. As in 1915 he had crushed Serbia, in 1916 occupied two-thirds of Roumania, so this year he fell upon the Italians at Caporetto on the 25th October. This enormous disaster, which cost the Italians 250,000 prisoners and a third of their artillery, brought the Austro-Germans by the beginning of November to the banks of the Piave, and it was decided that British and French forces should be dispatched to Italy to defend Venice and to give the Italian Army a breathing space for reorganisation. Therefore, when we were resting on the 21st, and speculating on the possibility of taking part in the Cambrai Battle so dramatically begun the day before, orders arrived for entrainment next afternoon with nine days' rations. The journey was made in two trains, under the command of Colonel Clarke and Major Aldworth respectively, which made for Italy by different routes, after leaving Troyes. Colonel Clarke's train reached Dijon on the second evening; Lyons early the next morning; throughout that day the exquisite and fruitful Rhone Valley passed before the delighted eyes of the men. The journey was slow, and when Avignon was reached at 2 a.m.

on the 25th, the train was already twelve hours late. Still further time was then lost owing to an accident at Toulon, which station was only entered at dusk after a triumphant progress through crowds of excited southerners, who gathered along the line cheering and waving. Most of the famous places of the French Riviera were passed in darkness, but at 8.10 on the 26th the frontier was passed at Ventimille. The journey continued along the lovely Italian coast until Savona was reached at nightfall. The Italians showed little disposition to welcome their deliverers, and the unpopularity of the war in these districts was patent. Next dawn found the train at Pavia, whence it proceeded along the Po to Cremona, where a 16-hour halt enabled the men to stretch their legs. With band playing they marched through the streets, and succeeded in arousing the enthusiasm of the inhabitants. The local commandante, Cav. Vittorio, a very courteous gentleman, took the salute as the two Companies re-entered the station. The extreme congestion of the Italian railways now upset all timetables completely. Mantua was not reached until 1 a.m. on the 29th, but finally the two Companies detrained at Saletto; and in the afternoon billeting orders arrived, and the evening found them lodged in a private house, a theatre and a monastery at Noventa. The billets were shared with a detachment of the Italian Veterinary Corps, the miserable condition of whose horses and mules bore witness to the rigours of the recent retreat. An 8-mile march next day over roads slippery with frost ended in a most elegant billet, a gorgeous château, which belonged to a Colonel Cabely, killed near Gorizia. Part of its magnificence, however, consisted in marble floors, a cold bed for men wrapped up in only one blanket.

Major Aldworth's train travelled more rapidly; by midnight on the 24th it had crossed the Mont Cenis and was running through Italian territory. Early next morning everyone was peering out of the windows at the great snow mountains through which the train descended to the Piedmontese Plain. The bells of the village churches were ringing everywhere on this Sunday morning as the train moved towards Turin, which was reached at noon on the 25th November. This city provided a rousing welcome; ladies handed out chocolate, cigarettes and little silk flags from the platform; the train steamed out into the open country between vociferating crowds. The journey henceforth was slow and circuitous, the direction being first north-east to Milan, which was passed during the night of 26th-27th November; then south to Pavia, and from there along the Po through Mantua to Nogaro, where the men were comfortably installed in billets by 9 p.m. on 27th November. Both journeys were as comfortable as could be expected in the exceptional circumstances. The men were able to get a hot drink at least twice a day, which was often supplemented by the energy of Red Cross ladies on the platforms, particularly in France.

CHAPTER 20

The Italian Winter

Happy the Battalion which for a while at least in wartime has no history. We had come to Italy expecting at once to be desperately engaged against the victorious invaders. But the Italians, greatly to their credit, had reorganised their broken forces, and, with their left resting on the mountains, had repelled all attempts of the enemy to cross the Piave, swollen with autumn rains. By the end of December the British and French Armies were fully concentrated, and a period of immobility set in, not to be broken for six months. The 48th Division, which formed part of General Haking's 11th Corps, found itself peacefully installed in Army Reserve. Under the clear Italian skies, in the peaceful Venetian plain, moderately well housed and not overworked, their lot was cast in a fair ground. The two halves of the Battalion reunited on 4th December, and finally settled on the 15th December at S. Croce Bigolina, where they remained six weeks. This village is situated just east of the Brenta, about 20 miles north of Padua, where G.H.Q. were established, and a similar distance south of the foothills of the Trentino Alps, where the line ran through the famous plateau of Asiago. Excursions to these hills in small parties for the purpose of reconnaissance formed from time to time a diversion from the ordinary routine of training.

Christmas was celebrated with great festivity. The officers had supplemented the men's rations by a subscription, stores were purchased in Vicenza and Padua, and a cheque of £50 was received from the County Association for the same purpose. Dinners, concerts and suppers were provided for the Companies; the officers were given free use of the house of the Parish Priest, who was entertained by them as the guest of the evening. It was the happiest Christmas which had been spent overseas.

With the New Year winter set in with a hard, bright frost, so keen that all the running streams were frozen. Visits of inspection were paid by General Plumer, the popular Commander-in-Chief, and by General Haking, whose kindliness and geniality in chatting to the men as individuals was heartily welcomed. At this time also the gratifying news was received that the commanding officer had been awarded the C.M.G.

On the 24th January the Battalion left S. Croce amidst general regret. The excellent priest, who had worked with all his will to promote good relations, in a parting message to Colonel Clarke especially commended the honourable and chivalrous relations which had existed between the troops and the women of the neighbourhood. At Paviola, which was reached after a weary march in a misty thaw over roads reduced to quagmires, the Battalion split up again: B and D Companies, with Headquarters remained in the same area, while Captain Challenor with the remainder moved to the Convent di Praglia, south of Padua, in order to supply working parties to the central school at G.H.Q. Here they remained till the end of February, doing every kind of job, to the complete satisfaction of those concerned. Some worked at the quarries, some at a bayonet-fighting assault course, some at the musketry school, others at the gas school; finding, however, time between their labours to play a number of football matches with neighbouring units.

By the end of the month all were again reunited; their long spell of rest had come temporarily to an end, and on the 27th they took over from the 2nd Queen's (7th Division) reserve lines on the Montello, that well-known hill overlooking the right bank of the Piave, which was one of the key-positions of the Italian line. The next fortnight was spent in this area, about half in the front line. It was an interesting though, fortunately, not a very dangerous experience, as the losses amounted only to one killed and one wounded. The long hill, which stretched for miles to the west of the river, was furrowed with numbers of deep, narrow dells, in which the platoons were housed. Along the foreshore was a series of disconnected posts, every second of which was armed with a Lewis gun. The majority of these were held only at night. They looked across the wide bed of the Piave, which, like all capricious mountain streams, divided into three or four channels, intersected by overgrown islands and beds of shingle, which heavy rain, as in the June battles, would convert speedily into a roaring torrent. The widest and deepest stream flowed on the enemies' side. Their inactivity was very marked, scarcely a shot was fired either by day or night, and except for the last day their artillery gave few signs of life. As was proved time after time, the last thing desired by the weary and disillusioned Austrian was to provoke the British. This interlude was the nearest approach to warfare encountered for many weeks to come. On the night of the 14th March in intense darkness the Italians relieved us without incident, and we turned our backs on the Montello for good. The division now moved west for many days; some short time was spent at Arsego, but it was not till 3rd April that the Battalion settled down to a three weeks' sojourn at Valle, in the hill country west of

Vicenza. The great events, which were shaking the Western Front to its foundations, found no echo here; two British Divisions were, it is true, moved to France, but the 48th was not among them. The Austrians as yet showed no signs of renewing their attacks.

While the Battalion were at Valle they lost their Commanding Officer, Lieut.-Colonel Clarke, who was appointed to command the newly-formed Divisional Machine Gun Battalion. His departure was deeply regretted. He had led the Battalion through all its serious fighting, and had gained the complete confidence of all. He had kept a strict discipline without worrying the men about trifles; they could all appreciate his administrative ability, his grasp of detail and practical concern for their comfort. We were fortunate in gaining as his successor Colonel Lloyd Baker, of the Bucks Battalion, who had been well-known earlier in the war as General McClintock's Staff Captain, and he brought to his new duties all his characteristic kindness and tact.

Meanwhile the constant exercise in hill-climbing for men and pack ponies, the schemes of attack and defence suggested that our next destination would be northward in the mountains. Nor was expectation falsified; for by the 23rd the Battalion had climbed up out of the warm, showery spring of the valley, and billeted in Italian huts at Granezza, about 4,500 feet above sea-level in storms of snow and hail. They were in Brigade Reserve immediately behind the lines on the Asiago plateau, which they were destined to guard until the advance to final victory at the end of October.

CHAPTER 21

Mountain Warfare

The new line ran along the forward slope of the hills, which had just been so painfully climbed, and whose reverse sides sheltered in their folds, densely populated with pine forests, the local reserves. The trenches themselves were strangely unlike any as yet inhabited, being blasted out of the solid rock. An impressive and, indeed, magnificent panorama extended itself in front. The valley of the Seven Communes, that curious little tongue of German-speaking territory projecting into pre-war Italy, ran across the foreground. Barren and almost treeless, it had been in the battle-line since the Austrian offensive of May, 1916, which had nearly broken successfully into the Venetian plain. Many villages and hamlets dotted the plain, especially towards the western end, the most imposing of which was Asiago. Though knocked about to a certain extent, they offered a regular and habitable outline as compared with the blank desolation of France. On the further side of the valley the pine-clad shoulders of the mountains were gradually merged in the great snow-covered, cloud-capped bastions of the Alps. Between the lines a vast No Man's Land extended, in many places nearly a mile in width, with miniature hills and valleys, and studded with houses and copses, over which our patrols were able to roam almost at will unmolested. Such was the general calm prevailing that officers in the front line were accustomed to sleep in their pyjamas. The entire casualties during May, most of which month was spent in the line, were three wounded. In a successful raid carried out on the 12th by two platoons of D Company, 2nd Lieut. Stott, slightly wounded, was the only victim. He obtained the M.C. and the Italian Silver Medal for Valour as a reward for his work. It was somewhat difficult to capture the prisoner required for identification, as the only post encountered promptly ran away; one, however, of the elderly Hungarians of the 24th Honved Regiment, who composed it, tripped and fell into a shell-hole, and was carried off by the raiders. The enemy made up for their lack of resistance by bombing their own wire and shouting assiduously until daybreak. On the 22nd the Battalion returned to Cornedo, in the plains; summer had by now fully set in; the vines, the maize, the mulberry and the orange, with many other diverse forms of luxuriant foliage, had completely changed the aspect of the country. The men were glad to wear the suits of drill and the sun-helmet which had now been issued. Thus May merged into June; the fourth great German attack was battering at the gates of Compiègne, but the Italian front had as yet given no sign. On our next visit, however, to the line, it became known that a British offensive was to be launched in the middle of June. The usual conferences and rehearsals took place; detailed orders were issued, the very date became known. It was to take place on the 16th of June. Twenty-four hours beforehand the Austrians, goaded at length out of their long sleep by the prodding of their Allies, suddenly launched that great attack on practically the whole of the front, which was the last offensive effort of the Hapsburg dynasty. After a somewhat alarming initial success on the Montello and the lower Piave, it changed into a complete failure. We have now to see how it affected the fortunes of our Battalion.

The Austrian attack was planned after the model of Ludendorf's great offensive of March 21st; that is to say, it was preceded by a short but violent bombardment of high explosive and gas directed particularly on the back areas and gun-positions. Its effectiveness was not, however, great, partly owing to the extreme difficulty of searching all the crannies of the mountain country, partly because the level of Austrian efficiency was low. Their gas-shells, in particular, seem to have been almost innocuous. The shelling began about 3 a.m., and lasted for three hours, when the infantry left the trenches. The two British Divisions in the line, 23rd and 48th, were attacked by portions of four Austrian Divisions; it is said that the latter had been brought up immediately before the battle in lorries, and told that their objective was weakly held by Italians, as their disinclination to face British and French troops was notorious. However that may be, they advanced against our Division with considerable energy at the outset. The two Battalions of the 145th Brigade in the line were from right to left, the 1st/4th Oxfords and 1st/5th Gloucesters. The enemy succeeded in driving in the outer flanks of both Battalions, and also in pushing a wedge between them to a maximum depth of about 1,000 yards. But attacking uphill over unfamiliar and blind country, exposed to cross-fire from rifles and machine-guns, and heavily bombarded, their progress was soon arrested. Our Battalion was in Brigade Reserve, and did useful work during the day in joining hands with the two assaulted Battalions. D Company joined the Oxfords at noon, and suffered some loss during the afternoon while forming up in the open to counter-attack. Here its commander, Captain C. Buck, a good and conscientious officer, was killed. He had served unhurt through the whole of the third Battle of Ypres, and was the only officer whom we lost by death during the Italian year.

Next morning very early, with the co-operation of C Company and one platoon of A, a completely successful advance was made to the old front line. All the heart had now gone out of the enemy, the failure of whose effort was patent. They made scarcely a shadow of resistance, and more than 60 prisoners remained in our hands. During the previous day C Company had been already engaged in stopping the gap between the Oxfords and Gloucesters. The latter, who had been isolated on both flanks, were in danger of complete encirclement during the morning and early afternoon, but extricated themselves and joined hands with C Company at 5.30 p.m.

During the 16th the whole divisional front was without exception re-established, and patrols were pushed forward into No Man's Land; the Austrians continued to surrender in little bodies, until the Division had collected over 1,000, with eight mountain guns abandoned and picked up. The casualty list of the Battalion afforded happy proof of the ineffectiveness of the enemy. We lost no more than five killed and 13 wounded. Thus ended ignominiously the great Austrian attack.

CHAPTER 22

The Last Summer

The remainder of June was spent pleasantly in rest billets, disturbed only by the first of the great influenza epidemics, which, pursuing a mild course, resulted in no deaths, but caused the evacuation in all of 112 men. On the 20th the Division lost their Commander, Sir R. Fanshawe, who returned home. He had commanded us for more than three years; devoted to the care of his Division and to the task of defeating the enemy, he demanded in everything the same high standard which he always set himself. A frequent visitor to the trenches, he did not reserve his appearance for quiet times; at Pozières and Ronssoy, for example, he was on the captured ground at the heels of his infantry. Therefore, he retained the confidence of the men throughout, in good days and bad.

Our sojourn in the plains was prolonged during the first twenty days of July under the full heat of summer, all moves being made in the early hours of the morning. On 12th July the Battalion had the satisfaction of winning the Divisional Signal Competition.

The ten days spent in the line were devoid of incident, one man only being wounded by a shell, and on the 30th July a return was made to Marziele for ten days, where a terrific storm one night blew down all the tents and bivouacs. The 10th August found them again in the mountains taking over from the 6th Gloucesters the extreme left of the divisional line. The war had now entered upon its penultimate stage with the splendid Allied victories of 18th July and 8th August; the enemy had lost everywhere the initiative, and was not to have the chance of regaining it. Although the Italians did not feel themselves capable at present of any important attack, the Austrians were not left in peace. Large-scale raids resulting often in the capture of hundreds of prisoners, were undertaken without respite by the French and British, provoking no attempt at retaliation.

Nor was the Battalion without share in these activities. The ground was first prepared for a full-dress raid by offensive patrols. On August 16th Lieut. Baxton attacked and bombed a party of the enemy on Coda Spur, the bombs falling clean among them. On the 15th a similar party under 2nd Lieut. Crawford shot five Austrians, who were patrolling their own wire, and who, when challenged, with fatal stupidity, halted and stood outlined against the skyline, an easy mark.

The time was now ripe for a more ambitious effort. The Battalion was withdrawn for a few days to Granezza, and returning to the trenches on the evening of the 26th, made a successful raid that same night in conjunction with the Bucks on our left. The attack was to be directed against the enemy trenches on either side of Asiago, the point of junction between the Battalions being at the south-east corner of the town. All four Companies were engaged; C on the right was to form a defensive flank within the enemy's trenches; B, on the left, was to seize the front line before Asiago, where A, passing through, would secure the support line, and allow D Company in turn, passing through them, to explore the southernmost limits of the town, and join hands with the Bucks. The withdrawal was to be in inverse order—*i.e.*, C and B were to hold the captured positions until the other two Companies had been safely passed back. Zero hour was 10.40 p.m., and there had been no preliminary barrage. The Companies had moved out from our outpost line at 9 p.m. and got into striking position after safely traversing the wide intervening area. As they lay waiting for the fiery signal, the enemy began to show nervousness; they had probably heard something suspicious, but could not see far, as clouds obscured the moon, and a white mist hung in the valley. They fired lights and rifle grenades and a few shells during the last half-hour before the bombardment opened, but caused no serious inconvenience. The barrage worked well; 32 minutes elapsed before it completed its shift from the front line to the final objective, which also it enclosed in a frame of shells on either flank. Here it remained for one hour, after which it died gradually away, as the withdrawal progressed. C Company reached and held their objective on the right with little difficulty, extracting 50 prisoners from the trenches and dugouts. B were equally successful, though a little hand-to-hand fighting was necessary to force an entrance on their right; they found the trenches shallow and ruinous, with few occupants (they could only collect six prisoners), and the dugouts in the quarry behind were wholly untenanted. The enemy annoyed them during their occupation of the trench with continuous shell-fire. A Company, according to programme, now passed through them in small columns, but as their commander was hit at this difficult moment, they lost direction and got mixed up with the Bucks, so that only one platoon met the enemy, who showed some fight in houses and dugouts near his support line. D Company successfully reached their objective, the enemy flying wildly before them and leaving four only in their hands. Those houses of Asiago which they searched were neither garrisoned nor fortified. The withdrawal took place with surprising ease, without even being troubled by systematic shell-fire. Prisoners were handed in to the 144th Brigade and receipts were given for 72; but it seems that nearly 100 was the actual bag. Casualties were fairly numerous, amounting in all to 77, but very light in character, only one man being killed and four missing, while of the wounded 26 remained on duty. The majority of wounds was due to shell-fire and unaimed machine-gun bullets, as there was very little genuine fighting. Many awards were made in connection with this well-executed operation; they are given in an appendix. I may mention here that Captain Cawley, who was wounded, received the M.C. and the Italian Silver Medal, and C.S.-M. Alder the same Italian decoration, together with the D.C.M.

September passed quite quietly in alternations between the front line and Granezza. The Battalion was now under the command of Colonel Whitehead, who succeeded, but did not replace, Colonel Lloyd Baker. He was a brave man, but of a narrow and unsympathetic school, staled by continuous service throughout the war.

October brought no change except in the weather, which declined suddenly to autumn on the hilltops, with night-frosts and continuous violent rain. The Austrians were still harassed perpetually by enormous and invariably successful raids, by bombardments and aerial bombing, to which they submitted with the patience of necessity.

The absence of any great concerted attempt to destroy them seemed almost inexplicable to our troops, as they heard of all the great works which were being performed against their enemies elsewhere. Already had Bulgaria fallen; the last Turkish Army had been dissolved; the German line was crumbling to pieces under the remorseless hammer of the British; and the interchange of Notes with America foreshadowed the end of the war. The Italians, however, were determined to wait until the possibility of failure had been reduced to a minimum, and doubtless they were the best judges of the capacity of their own troops. Thus it was not until 25th October that they launched the blow which was to prove the destruction of the Austrian Empire.

CHAPTER 23

Victory

The attack was started first on the Piave and the Brenta; and operations further west were contingent on success in those areas. Accordingly, its effects did not become apparent on our front until 29th October, when the Austrians were already in headlong flight towards the Tagliamento. At that date we were holding the extreme right of the Divisional Area. On that morning, at daybreak, C Company sent out a patrol, which found that the Austrians had abandoned their front lines—a retirement which deserters had foreshadowed for some days past. They pushed on at noon and entered Asiago, a silent village; thence exploring more boldly, they wandered right across the valley as far as Ebene, close to its northernmost limits. There they saw the French patrols similarly engaged in searching the houses. Then the enemy gave the first sign of his continued existence, firing with two machine guns from a little knoll, which commanded the village 500 or 600 yards away. The Bucks, who were out on the left, brought back similar word, and it was apparent that a general retirement had been carried out to their Winterstellung, or Winter Lines, which ran along the northern slopes and barred ingress into the side valleys which led up to the railway of the Val Sugana. It now became necessary to discover whether the enemy was standing strongly in this main line of defence, or whether it could be overrun by a *coup-de-main*. During the night of the 29th-30th, therefore, B Company was sent forward to feel its way and report on the resistance encountered. Captain Winslow now established his Headquarters in the Military Barracks at Asiago, keeping one platoon at hand. The remaining three spread widely over the plain and moved forward. They occupied the villages lying at the foot of the mountains, but it was evident that the enemy was still in strength before them. Here and there they extracted Austrians who had been left behind in houses and dugouts. The left platoon, in particular, discovered 17 in Bosco, including an officer; as they drove this party before them towards Asiago, while it was still light, machine-gun fire was directed upon them from the ridges of Monte Catz, causing several casualties. The prisoners, headed by their officer, were foolish enough to refuse to continue their journey, and their mutiny cost them dear, as, with one exception, they were all killed. Next day A Company took on the patrolling work, and found the lines still occupied, while the Austrians denied them access to Costa, which had been examined on the previous day. Reports from either flank gave similar information; there was nothing, therefore, to suggest the speedy and dramatic overthrow which was to follow.

During the night of the 31st October-1st November, the Corps decided to make a general attack at dawn, the orders being verbally delivered to Colonel Whitehead by the Brigade-Major soon after midnight. There was thus very little time to make preparations. Fortunately Major Battcock was acting as intelligence officer, and set to work with all his characteristic energy and method. He had only rejoined the Battalion at his own request some days previously, and although senior to every officer except that of the Colonel, had volunteered to act in any capacity in which he could be useful. He was living in advanced Headquarters at Asiago School, and succeeded in getting everyone in position by 3.30 a.m. Meanwhile D Company, whose duty it was that night to patrol in front, reported that Monte Catz was still strongly held. This long bare shoulder, which projected southward from the main ridge into the valley, was the objective of the Battalion. It was the key of the whole of this section of the Winterstellung, as it overlooked the trenches on either side. At 5.35 the attack was launched; C and D Companies, from right to left, were charged with the assault; they advanced close behind a barrage. Each had a section widely extended in advance as skirmishers, the main body advancing in two lines. C Company met with immediate and splendid success. Brushing aside opposition at Costa and on the slopes of the hill, they stood upon the summit at 7.30 a.m.; they had already taken 65 prisoners and had completely cleared their area. D Company had met with a tougher resistance, and being assailed by cross-fire from both right and left, were held up in the Plain until B Company came into the gap, and seized the machine-gun nests on the south-west slopes of Monte Catz about 7.30 a.m.

Thus our position was satisfactory beyond expectation. The 144th Brigade, however, on the left, were in a less happy condition. Their assault on the lower slopes of M. Interrotto had not been successful. The enemy had even passed to a counter-offensive, and had thrown them back beyond the uttermost villages of the Plain, Camporovere and Bosco. The evacuation of the latter imperilled all our dispositions, and Colonel Whitehead wisely kept A Company at Asiago in case the enemy should drive a wedge between the two Brigades. It was the more unfortunate that O.C. D Company, acting on one of those vague orders which often circulate during battle, whose source it is impossible to trace with certainty, had withdrawn his company some-what from the slopes, believing himself to be conform-ing to the desires of the 144th Brigade. Monte Catz was therefore left in a dangerously salient position on the west, but as the Bucks, and beyond them the French on the east, had been completely successful, it was thought well to take the risk of exploiting the success which the 145th Brigade had already won. The indefatigable C Company, therefore, pushed on up the hill, seized and passed the Sichestal Trench (the last organised defence in that area); the Bucks securely protected their right flank; on the left B Company held a line slanting backwards to the Plain, where D continued the line on the outskirts of Bosco, still untaken. All this was accomplished by about 3 p.m. The blow of the Battalion had been decisive, as Lord Cavan mentions in his despatch. They had taken that day 480 prisoners, and more than 30 guns, and had destroyed many more. Next morning the 144th Brigade seized all their objectives with little difficul-ty; the Winterstellung existed no longer. The Division held the entrance and both sides of the Val d'Assa, and began to march up it towards their final objective, the Val Sugana, one of the main nerves of the enemy system. The Austrians fell into a rout, which can have few parallels in military history. Famished and without hope in the world, faced at the same moment with military disaster and political collapse, they fled headlong into the mountains, or swarmed down in enormous numbers to surrender to our advancing troops; almost the last remnant of self-respect which they retained was their determination not to become the prisoners of the Italians. The rough mountain tracks were blocked with their debris; and the crowds of unarmed men embarrassed our advance-guards and checked their progress. Generals and superior officers came down to meet us, sometimes at the head of troops, sometimes as solitary stragglers. A Corps

Commander and three Divisional Generals were among the spoil of the Division. Here and there during the 2nd and the early morning of the 3rd, little bodies of devoted men still resisted; as at Mount Meatta, where a Company of 4th Oxfords put 100 Austrians to flight after a sharp combat. It was noted also that when the red-capped Bosnian Regiment surrendered to our Battalion, the men obeyed their officers smartly, and laid down their arms and equipment neatly at the word of command. It was curious that these Mahommedans, from the latest acquired of all the Austrian possessions, should have been the most faithful to their military oath. During the 3rd the confusion among the Austrians was, if possible, increased by their mistaken belief that the Armistice had come into force; they ceased even the isolated semblance of resistance, and were herded in the valleys like sheep. Meanwhile the Division advanced inexorably by the Val d'Assa and the subsidiary Val Portule; they crossed the enemy's frontier at 8.30 on that morning, first of all the armies of the West (except for that portion of Alsace which had remained in French hands since 1914). That evening the Battalion lodged in Caldonazza, just south of the Val Sugana; here the enemy had abandoned a vast ordnance park and more than 200 guns. The Advanced Guards were already in Levico, that pleasant little spa in the valley, with its baths and springs, only 20 miles from Trent. Next morning the news came that the Armistice was signed and was to come into force at 3 p.m. The weary troops continued their march up the valley until that hour, taking still vast quantities of prisoners; then they halted. For our Battalion the war ended at the village of Vigalzano. They had covered 35 miles in two and a-half days over rough paths in the mountains. Not a single man had fallen out. Their casualties in this last glorious battle amounted to 17 killed and 23 wounded. Their individual captures cannot be recorded, but the booty of the Division was unprecedented, and reached 22,000 prisoners and at least 600 guns.

Here I will leave them; I will not describe their subsequent stay in Italy, the demobilisation of the Battalion, the return of the nucleus and its welcome at Reading, or its rebirth in peace under its present popular and capable Commander, Colonel Aldworth, and its excellent Adjutant, Captain Goodenough.

Let us not forget these Berkshire men, who played a worthy part in the changing scenes of this tremendous conflict: who, at the close, amidst the utter confusion of their enemies, bore witness to the truth of that saying, 'He that endureth to the end, the same shall be saved.'

Appendices

Appendix A

1/4TH BATTALION ROYAL BERKSHIRE REGIMENT
ROLL OF OFFICERS, NON-COMMISSIONED OFFICERS AND MEN WHO
DIED IN THE WAR

CAPTAINS
Attride, R. G.
Buck, C.
Down, W. O., M.C.

LIEUTENANTS
Hunt, N. G.
Palmer, R. W. P.
Ridley, L. E.

SECOND-LIEUTENANTS
Bartram, A.
BEASLEY, A. W., M.M.
Clayton, N.
Garside, T. O.
Heppell, H. D.
Teed, H. S.
Wakeford, G. T.

ATTACHED TO OTHER UNITS
Lieut.-Colonel Thorne, H. U. H.
Lieut. Wells, H. M. W.

COMPANY SERGT.-MAJORS
392 Lawrence, W.
200546 Wright, A. T., D.C.M.

COMPANY QUARTERMASTER SERGEANTS
599 Moore, F. W.
1637 Perrin, C.

SERGEANTS
2399 Amor, A. S.
200627 Benn, C.
2478 Brewerton, W. W.
200485 Childs, F.
2327 Didcock, F.
2402 Forge, G. F.
202093 Garrard, C. J. C.
200080 Giles, F. C.
2883 Grant, E. J.
426 Haines, G.
891 Hedges, F. W.
203799 Henson, A.
2446 Hewett, W. C. E.
200010 Holloway, W. C.
2610 House, A. E.

169

200861 Lukeman, C. H.
2529 Lush, G.
200605 Nicholls, A.
200406 Paddick, H.
200670 Parker, C. J.
200169 Parker, J.
2773 Pinnell, H. J.
44 Reddrop, R. T.
200542 Russell, T. D.
441 Rutter, P.
2434 Taylor, V. H.
200246 Weavings, R.
200690 Wright, F. J.

LANCE-SERGEANTS
2342 Gorring, H. J.
200390 Langford, A. W.
1937 Watson, F. W.
200192 Webb, F. W.

CORPORALS
202402 Cocking, J. H. A.
200422 Davies, E. L., M.M.
2340 Jones, A. T. N.
12799 Killmaster, W.
201482 Knight, F.
1830 Painter, A. G.
2701 Papps, A. C.
2575 Piggott, W.
203840 Russell, W. J.
1678 Rutland, H. S.
1825 Searle, A. E.
203836 Simmonds, T. G.
200896 Snow, J. M.
2154 Taylor, W. G.
201555 Watts, W.
2395 Wilson, R. G.

LANCE-CORPORALS
200412 Attride, G. J.
200382 Barker, E. A.
200344 Beard, H. E.
2765 Boston, A. W.

200137 Brooks, A. C.
203198 Campbell, H.V.
5649 Cole, A. C.
200125 Cook, W. C.
200160 Dean, H. S.
1625 Deane, M. A. C.
200946 Dee, A. E.
2176 Garrett, F. H.
2947 George, R. W.
666 Godwin, A. H.
2946 Goodall, A.
200813 Hands, W. T.
3015 Haskins, R.
200513 Hatto, H. H.
2659 House, H. J.
203833 Jenkins, W.
4945 Johnson, W. G. A.
1470 Lambert, A. J.
1767 Legge, A. E.
201450 Lewis, F. C.
200242 Mills, G.
2442 Odell, E.V.
200425 Perkins, E. H. R.
201508 Rackley, A.
200621 Saunders, E.
6289 Smith, F.
1690 Somerville, S.
2354 Vaughan, F. W.
201543 Ward, E.
5775 Wright, A.V.

PRIVATES
4716 Abery, L. H.
5529 Adlam, F. C.
200545 Allum, F. S.
203061 Andrews, G.
202156 Andrews, W.
201477 Annetts, P.
5455 Appleton, G.
2653 Atkins, F.
200824 Aubrey, F. W.
201843 Austin, J. W.
5654 Ayles, E. H.

1883 Ayres, F.
714 Bacon, P. G. W.
1939 Badcock, A.
4682 Baker, P. G.
200617 Barnett, A. A.
1768 Barney, C.
5789 Bateman, J.
2962 Beckett, A. J.
5831 Beckinsale, L.
200157 Belcher, H.
200743 Belcher, S. E.
202211 Benger, A. T.
201877 Bickle, A. E.
5843 Bird, F.
1473 Blade, H. R. W.
4920 Bloomfield, C. I.
200472 Bolton, C.
10116 Bond, F. S.
2748 Boothby, R.
37969 Borley, F. G.
3088 Bowell, G. P.
20662 Bracey, G. G.
200400 Brant, B. J. L.
36259 Bromley, H.
5444 Brooman, H. B.
2076 Brown, C. J. F.
200544 Brown, S. R.
203847 Brown, W. A.
203181 Buckingham, F. J.
220192 Bullen, E. L.
18181 Burrows, C.
2782 Butler, A. J.
4969 Buxcey, A. E.
200960 Buxton, W.
200632 Cane, N.
203294 Cannon, H. F.
202033 Carter, A.
203195 Chaplin, F. A.
2122 Chapman, A. E.
202068 Chapman, W. J.
5327 Clarke, E. F.
36539 Clayton, W. M.
37974 Clements, F.

203192 Cleveland, F. T.
201991 Cockell, J.
5648 Collacott, F. E. V.
201548 Collis, A.
202139 Commins, H. J.
34087 Cook, A. E.
18346 Cook, F. H. V.
30435 Cook, J.
203706 Cook, R.
37977 Cooke, F. T.
5671 Cooper, H.
17723 Copas, A. W.
4801 Coventry, H. T.
4815 Cox, E. B.
5263 Coxhead, W.
5199 Cripps, A. E.
200902 Crook, W.
4701 Cropp, C.
5349 Cruse, A. G.
202219 Curtis, W. J.
202181 Dale, S.
2656 Dance, W. W. S.
202887 Darling, F. H.
5855 Davey, A. A.
2983 Denham, C. W.
2753 Dix, W. H.
5828 Dixon, G.
202230 Drake, F. J. V.
5738 Duckett, H. E.
202107 Eade, J.
202149 Eady, L.
200566 Early, F. W.
20350 Eighteen, H. T.
5083 Elbrow, A. J.
201908 Elwick, C. G.
201773 Emmett, C. W.
202186 Emmons, C. W. H.
5208 Evans, D.
200535 Fennell, F.
3250 Filbee, W. H. F.
3271 Filmore, H. W.
37921 Fisher, H. A.
203326 Fleetwood, F. P.

20202 Fleming, B.
2727 Ford, A. E.
200878 Freeman, J.
12384 Freeth, R.
202895 French, H.
201970 Fryer, E. G.
203712 Fullbrook, A. H.
37979 Furness, F. C.
203075 Garraway, R. H.
201356 Geater, A. J.
2539 Gee, R. B.
2996 Gibbard, H.
4983 Gibbons, C. E.
5641 Giles, E. S.
3053 Giles, F.
203881 Giles, H.
37915 Goddard, H. T. W.
200058 Goodenough, A. S. J.
2062 Goodship, A. B.
4874 Gore, A. J.
201412 Gould, A.
4939 Grant, G.
44411 Grant, G.
5131 Graves, T. H.
203255 Green, W. G.
32808 Greenaway, E.
5092 Greenough, E. J.
4124 Grigg, J.
201694 Haines, A. E.
201757 Haines, H. W.
2613 Hall, A. E.
201883 Hall, A. E.
201883 Harding, A. E.
203727 Harmer, H.
2723 Harris, J. F.
2881 Harvey, E. E.
4759 Harvey, F. W.
203793 Hawkes, C. J.
5178 Hays, J.
2968 Head, W.
1686 Heath, W. H.
2130 Herne, G.
200660 Herring, C.

201736 Hester, H. R.
5688 Higgins, A. H.
2380 Higgs, A. W.
201085 Higgs, J.
202365 Hill, S. A.
36755 Hipkiss, J. P.
202201 Hodges, S. G.
202426 Holloway, E.
4906 Holton, F. V.
37918 Hood, J.
202247 Hopkins, R. G.
2718 House, O.
203852 Humphries, W.
3382 Hunt, A.
203736 Ireland, G.
37186 Jackson, C.
202044 Jefferies, G. H.
37958 Jessel, H.
37939 Jones, L. L.
201568 Jones, T. H.
200293 Josey, B.
200196 Kinchin, H.
203187 King, A. E.
6126 King, F.
201455 King, H. A.
2616 Knott, A. T.
200251 Lambourne, W.
200834 Langford, A. B.
203746 Langmead, A. R.
6124 Lee, A. H.
202016 Lennard, J.
202041 Leonard, A.
3058 Leonard, R.
202703 Lett, G. E.
3113 Lewendon, A.
5709 Liddard, E.
200291 Long, D.
2607 Loving, H.
2204 Luke, W. S.
200783 Lunnon, P.
36028 Macdonald, A.
37913 Main, A. H.
3955 Maidwaring, H.

3198 Marshall, H. K.
202124 Martin, J.
36831 Mason, L. G. A.
203045 Mathers, G.
3166 May, C.
202118 May, P.
3836 McKay, J.
3060 Meads, F.
3809 Meads, T.
201494 Meads, W. H.
14102 Merriman, H. J. C.
203817 Miles, W. H.
1816 Miles, W. T. G.
18439 Millest, S. E.
200583 Mitcham, W. C.
41312 Mitchell, G.
2758 Moody, L. F.
5422 Morton, T. W.
2951 Muggridge, F. J.
2143 Mulford, F.
200361 Mulford, R. C. A.
37932 Nacowitz, J.
201396 Neale, G. W.
3193 Nelson, F.
200099 New, J.
37941 Newell, J.
20375 Newman, E. T.
1826 Noakes, A.
200454 Norman, J. P.
201765 Osborne, H. J.
201994 Packford, C.
3483 Painter, F. C.
202194 Panting, G. A.
5240 Parker, A. Y.
203760 Parker, H. L.
5653 Parsons, C. F.
5567 Parsons, W. H.
202148 Pascoe, H.
201839 Pearce, E. A.
201474 Pearce, W. A.
36417 Pepper, C.
3234 Piddington, W. J.
3456 Pike, W.

37960 Platt, R.
202014 Plumridge, W.
3032 Pocock, S. H. V.
201029 Pocock, S. R.
200310 Poole, J. H.
2713 Pratt, R. E.
36684 Prowse, W.
203846 Quarterman, C. F.
3450 Rackley, F.
202892 Robertson, R. H.
4974 Robey, W. R.
37169 Robinson, C. E.
6144 Rodman, S. H.
3004 Rogers, G. F. D.
2057 Rose, C. R.
18532 Rudge, S.
200373 Russ, E.
201581 Sadler, J. H.
203803 Sadler, T.
3384 Salmon, H.
35971 Salmon, W. H.
37989 Sargent, S.
200737 Schaffer, A.
201975 Searing, A.
202059 Searle, C.
202121 Searle, E.
2848 Selby, F. P.
2845 Seymour, A. J.
3033 Shackleford, A. F.
201881 Sharland, H.
201801 Shepherd, C.
37935 Skuce, W.
2469 Smith, A. F.
2378 Smith, W. T.
37925 Spice, A. F.
21830 Stevens, L.
203854 Stratford, W.
2635 Street, H. S.
5312 Swain, A. T.
36875 Taylor, G.
202165 Tellan, F. E.
203822 Thompson, J. H.
203781 Thorn, R. E.

5164 Tipping, H.
202174 Trather, E.
203782 Treadwell, W. S.
200054 Turner, F.
2639 Turner, J.
203300 Tyler, W.
1751 Tyrell, E.
5193 Vickers, J.
5729 Vockins, B. O.
200879 Waite, A.
2960 Walker, H.V.
201060 Walters, C. H.
3216 Warren, P.
1947 Webb, G.W.
2017 Webb, W. E.
203845 Welch, F.A.
5844 Wells, A.
19430 Werrell, W.
203770 Wheatcroft, A. F.
5197 Wheeler, F.
1457 Wheeler, G.

200986 White, C.V.T.
2662 White, J. H.
4795 White, R. J.
5856 Whittle, W.
200804 Wickens, B. E.
200665 Wicks, N. J.
5143 Wicks, W. C.
5553 Wicks, W. G.
201131 Wiggins, A. J.
202115 Wiles, F.
5638 Williams, A. G.
5412 Wiltshire, G.
2580 Wing, A. G.
2633 Winter, L.V.
201514 Witts, H.
2764 Woodall, R. E.
202000 Woodley, A. G.
203790 Woodley, F. W.
202684 Woodward, H.
23660 Woolford, E. J.
5793 Young, S.

Appendix B

1/4TH BATTALION ROYAL BERKSHIRE REGIMENT
HONOURS AND DECORATIONS GAINED BY OFFICERS, N.C.O.'S AND MEN WHILE SERVING WITH THE BATTALION

C.M.G.
Colonel O. Pearce Serocold
Lieut.-Col. R. J. Clarke

D.S.O.
Lieut.-Col. A. B. Lloyd-Baker
Lieut.-Col. R. J. Clarke
Capt. W. A. Wetherilt

M.C.
Major J. N. Aldworth
Capt. S. Boyle
Capt. G. M. Gaythorne-Hardy
Capt. O. B. Challenor
Capt. W. O. Down
Capt. D. J. Ward
Capt. O. M. James
Capt. E. W. Crust
Capt. B. F. Holmes
Capt. J. W. Cawley
Capt. G. C. W. Gregory
Capt. L. Ball
Capt. L. T. Goodenough
Capt. S. C. Larn
Lieut. W. O. Forder

Lieut. P. G. Handford
Lieut. T. Rogers
Lieut. A. O. Stott
Lieut. H. T. Wevill
2nd/Lieut. E. E. Millar
200005 C.S.M., A. G. Rider
201108 C.S.M., W. H. Heath

DISTINGUISHED CONDUCT MEDAL
200024 R.S.M. Laidler, A. H.
200546 Sergt. Wright, A. T.
3134 Sergt. Rogers, T.
65 Sergt. White, S.
203794 Sergt. Gilding, F.
200569 Sergt. White, W. T.
405 Sergt. Westall, A. G.
200034 Sergt. Roberts, W. A.
201115 Sergt. Wilson, W.
200052 Sergt. Holloway, T.
200756 Sergt. Salmon, J. H.
200500 Sergt. Moore, S. W.
203791 C.S.M. Alder, G.
4749 Pte. Appleby, J.
2594 Pte. Sadler, G.

MILITARY MEDAL

12 Sergt. Beasley, A. W.
445 Sergt. Wickens, R. A.
203809 L/Cpl. Ranscombe, W.
142 Sergt. Shorter, G.
2035 Pte. Sellwood, P.
3128 Pte. Ross, B. A.
4968 Pte. Wernham, H. W.
3120 L/Cpl. Rixon, W.
2439 L/Cpl. Davies, E. L.
2612 L/Cpl. Rice, R.
2646 Corpl. Cooke, W.
200814 Pte. Mitchell, R.
144 Pte. Smith, S.
2629 Pte. Russell, T.
1547 Sergt. Goodenough, L. T.
2768 Corpl. Crust, E. W.
200150 Sergt. Garrett, E. J.
200633 Pte. Lambden, R. E.
200426 Sergt. Millican, H.
200847 L/Cpl. De Gruchy, H.
200620 Sergt. Martin, S.
200647 Sergt. Seeley, C. L.
203875 L/Sergt. Baylis, L. G.
200661 L/Cpl. Slatter, S. G.
201824 Pte. Breadmore, F.
200846 Sergt. White, H. G.
200406 Sergt. Paddick, H.
200373 Pte. Russ, E.
200682 Sergt. Fuller, B. H.
20649 L/Cpl. Mazey, J.
2772 Pte. Hutchings, G. W.
2252 Sergt. Evans, A.
3143 Corpl. Hart, H.
1858 Pte. Oliver, M. W.
8362 Corpl. Allen, W.
200675 Sergt. Shaw, E.
200263 Sergt. Harman, C. H.
37317 Corpl. White, N. B.
200356 Corpl. Withers, A. V.
38157 Pte. Black, D.
203850 Corpl. Cripps, H. J.
201508 Pte. Rackley, A.

36644 Pte. Edmunds, F.
26031 L/Cpl. Lloyd, L. V.
203873 Sergt. Thatcher, A.
200905 Pte. Robinson, F. W.
201115 Sergt. Wilson, W.
36796 Pte. Cooksey, E. H.
202187 Pte. Disbury, C.
200500 Sergt. Moore, S. W.
200256 Corpl. Duncan, J. A.
1794 L/Cpl. Sargent, E. N.
1140 Sergt. Holloway, T.
203771 L/Cpl. Stratton, W. W.
37937 L/Cpl. Rogers, S.
200485 Corpl. Childs, F. W.
200562 Pte. Clare, H. H.
203812 L/Cpl. Parris, A. T.
201775 Pte. Cund, F.
201917 Pte. Curtis, C. W.
200796 Pte. Stokes, W. J.
201505 Sergt. Prior, S. C.
200215 Pte. Carter, A.
203772 Pte. Cartland, J.
200216 L/Cpl. Bricks, H. A.
203862 Pte. Wiggins, C. W.
201753 Pte. Evans, G.
201796 L/Cpl. Thomas, M.
200877 L/Cpl. Freeman, J.
34146 Pte. Tyrrell, F.
202165 Pte. Crouch, W. J.
202244 L/Cpl. Edwards, H. F.
21799 Pte. Brooks, F. J.
201383 Pte. Hopkins, F.
17048 Pte. Fisher, A.
201776 Corpl. Sturgess, A. H.

MERITORIOUS SERVICE MEDAL

200423 C.Q.M.S. Pitman, C. E.
200063 C.Q.M.S. Snarey, F. A.
200019 C.Q.M.S. Hatton, E. S.
200849 Sergt. Grover, F. R.
200549 Sergt. Morris, W. H.
203829 L/Cpl. Kurton, C.
203753 Pte. Meads, H. H.

Mentioned in Despatches

Colonel O. Pearce Serocold
Lieut.-Col. R. J. Clarke
Lieut.-Col. A. B. Lloyd-Baker
Major G. A. Battcock
Major J. N. Aldworth
Capt. A. G. M. Sharpe
Capt. G. M. Gaythorne-Hardy
Capt. R. G. Attride
Capt. O. B. Challenor
Capt. L. Ball
Capt. A. C. Hughes
Capt. O. M. James
Capt. F. Winsloe
Capt. W. A. Wetherilt
Lieut. R. A. Hogarth
Lieut. J. Payne
Lieut. R. W. Wells
2/Lieut. C. A. Freeman
R.S.M. Hanney, W. C.
R.S.M. Hogarth, R. A.
2361 R.Q.M.S. Borton, E.
200024 C.S.M. Laidler, A. H.
200427 Sergt. Gutteridge, A.
200756 Sergt. Salmon, J. H.
203798 Sergt. Neal, S.
200540 Sergt. Monney, J. T.
200084 Sergt. Palmer, F.
1179 Sergt. Beaver, H.
200532 Sergt. Higgs, W. A. E.
200848 Sergt. Gale, A.
200947 L/Sergt. Earle, W.
200072 Corpl. Eggleton, A. E.
200356 Corpl. Withers, A. V.
200415 Corpl. Peacock, W. J.
200040 Corpl. Poulter, E.
200275 Corpl. Croft, J.
899 Corpl. Collier, G. H.
203182 L/Cpl. Parris, L.
200810 L/Cpl. Shaw, A. E.

17048 Pte. Fisher, A.
202196 Pte. Hardy, T. E.
200562 Pte. Clare, H. H.
38172 Pte. Jukes, F.

French Croix de Guerre

Lieut.-Col. H. F. Whitehead
203842 Pte. Holley, P. F.

Belgian Croix de Guerre

200415 Corpl. Peacock, W. J.

Italian Silver Medal for Valour

Capt. J. W. Cawley
Capt. W. A. Wetherilt
Lieut. A. O. Stott
203791 C.S.M. Alder, G.

Italian Bronze Medal for Valour

Lieut. O. Buxton
203846 Sergt. Gilbey, O.
38157 Pte. Black, D.

Italian Croce di Guerra

Lieut.-Col. A. B. Lloyd-Baker
202235 Sergt. Hill, A. J.
200569 Sergt. White, W. T.
203850 Corpl. Cripps, H. J.
201753 Pte. Evans, G.
36796 Pte. Cooksey, E. H.

French Officier du Mérite d'Agricole

Lieut.-Col. R. J. Clarke

French Chevalier Du Mérite d'Agricole

Major J. N. Aldworth

www.ingramcontent.com/pod-product-compliance
Lightning Source LLC
Chambersburg PA
CBHW021103090426
42738CB00006B/479